Translated from Spanish into English of the original Novel "Invasion Silenciosa".

Dedication

This work of historical character I want to dedicate it first to God because despite having to start again from nothing, has never abandoned me and has kept in me the desire to live.

To my wife and my children, because in spite of the difficulties we have had to live, we have always remained united and they have been my source of inspiration.

And finally to my country, because this story has allowed me to measure how much love I can feel for the land where I was born.

Novel

INVASION IN THE SHADOWS

Raúl Alberto Díaz

How one country invaded another by indoctrinating its population

Novel

INVASION IN THE SHADOWS

Raúl Alberto Díaz

How one country invaded another by indoctrinating its population

Raul Alberto Diaz Journalist Writer, Author of Invasion in the Shadows, after escaping from his native Venezuela, he decides to write this reality fiction novel whose plot will freeze its readers and

allow them to know the framework created by the leaders of a stream of thoughts whose source of ideas exhausted with the advance of society and its third industrial revolution. The story tells how a nation was invaded silent and strategict, as a last resort after several attempts to do so by force for subjected to a transformation to which it always resisted.

This literary piece told by whoever was hostage in his country in the first coup attempt that early morning in 1992, leaves a warning to the nations of the world about the domination to which they may be subjected by economic groups that lurk in the dark.

Table of Contents

Prologue

For some time I have dedicated myself to analyze the diverse situations of nations like Venezuela and others, that have seen the massive mobilization of their population, due to political or economical situations, individual security, wars or hunger problems.

I make these socio-political analyses in a general way, trying to tie up the dots, and find the reasons of why the matter, because I am one of those who thinks that behind everything there is a movement that is provoking this alteration of the order as a whole. However, I pay special attention to the situation of Venezuela, the central country in the hemisphere, around which different situations revolve that keep the American area in suspense.

As in my case, many journalists have had to go out into the world in search of freedom or security. For this reason I have been able to spread my ideas and my position against the Tyranny that lives in the homeland of Bolivar. I have been able to use Social Networks to make ideas fly and sometimes this gives light to certain topics that many people not to do. The reasons; Maybe they do not want to appear in the arena or for commitments with groups or political parties. Or simply out of fear.

In this sense my wife began to motivate me and tell me that I should write and gather ideas...to contribute with a literary material by writing a book. My answer always was that that was projected from my time in the university. After all, I am an integral/Global Journalist, but with a literary background, speaking in academical terms. I got my degree like a writer in Zulia State University, mention printed journalism.

Writing had been a project I had in mind. On one occasion I heard the great Master "El Musiu Lacavalerie", a renowned figure of Journalism in Latin America, say that a man was a complete human being when, first he fathered children and had a family, second when he planted a tree and cultivated it and third when he wrote a book with the aim of leaving a legacy.
Now several factors were conjugated and that moment arrived. Running away from my country. No longer being able to practice journalism in Venezuela, the persecution and first imprisonment of my father, an honorable and impeccable man who has been blinded by a political project whose initial argument ended up being a deception. Subsequently the persecution of my brother as a Graphic Journalist, who in in a bad time, recorded a video filming criminal moments of the dictatorship in Venezuela and

then the harassment against me, have been sufficient elements to make the decision to create this novel, which goes from reality to fiction and beyond. If there is one thing that is certain, it is that what we have lived during these 20 years surpasses by a great deal the fiction.

In general, the Venezuelan family was dismembered. Today in Venezuela the family, as the first cell of society, has been destroyed. For these and many other reasons, the time has come to gather and tell so many ideas and loose truths and to concatenate all these links.   The time has simply come.

Introduction

For much of its history, the South American Republic has been the jewel that everyone has wanted to conquer. Since the independence era, it has had to defend itself against nations that have sought and at times succeeded, seize its wealth and treasures, and even to subdue its population. The country has been able to deal with these situations with intelligence and courage.

The South American country is one of the richest nations in the world, speaking in terms of natural resources, and as time passes more and more minerals are filling the chemical table of rich elements in matter for the development of peoples. Not only was it enough with oil, iron and steel, but also have been appearing little by little, more veins of Gold, Uranium, Diamonds, and more recently have been discovered minerals such as Coltan (Blue Gold) and Thorium (Thorum), natural elements used for communications technology, nuclear and space energy.

Unfortunately this fact has turned the country into that jewel that everyone wants to have. In this sense a transcendentally important event has occurred for the country, initiated since the decade of the 60's and is none other than the attempted invasion executed by "The Commander of the Island" and his government. A particular character with pretensions to expand his communist project and who, in those incipient attacks, tried to invade the country by force and through its coasts, at least this is reflected in the story supported by journalistic data.

Faced with this fact, the inhabitants of the locality known as Machurú reported to the authorities, and the intention of invasion was avoided through a confrontation that left a lamentable toll of 8 people dead, in addition to several injured.

This fact was carried to the Organization of American States (OAS), which is why and after complying with the protocols, the Organization made a formal claim to the government of the Island, but the latter adopted a position of rejection in the face of these accusations, alleging that they had no knowledge of the matter. From then on, the South American country broke off relations with the island, as a result of such aggression. Even though at that moment the situation did not go any further, after 30 years the island would achieve its objective.

According to data provided by high-ranking military personnel, who occupied first level positions within the last democratic government of Venezuela before the arrival of Hugo Chavez, the invasion of Venezuela was finally consumed, on this occasion through the infiltration and indoctrination of new military officers and media, who accompanied the 'Golpista de Sabaneta', both in the coup attempts, as after assuming power in elections whose abstention level was close to 55%.

This novel seeks to draw a segment of the contemporary history, not only of the country of Oil, but of the world, being able to apply this reflection to countries that by their wealth and bad governments are in the sight of any nation with an invading project. The cases of Nicaragua, Cuba or Venezuela, for example, are emblematic. Also, the existing situation in African countries, whose inhabitants suffer the effects of power in the hands of a few, have provoked mass migratory movements that have surpassed any expectation, including those reflected in the post-World War II period.

With the new models of aggression against nations, applied by people and organizations behind the scenes, and with the weak and incomplete unification of international legal models that allow the rescue of 'X' region, whose rulers provoke hunger and death, no nation is safe from suffering an invasion.

As if they were a kind of franchise, with updated structures, supported by the acquisition of mass media as a first step before executing any other and perfected over time, similar schemes are used in many parts of the world.

Sometimes they use the right as an argument, but sometimes the left. However, the ever-present common denominator is a political tool called "Populism", whose edge undoubtedly affects much more the peoples whose political actors become the worst representation of their interests and the reason why those masses see deception as their only way out.

Chapter 1

That morning

1992

Three in the morning. As every day, well actually from Monday to Friday, Rodolfo between the clock alarm, and the pats of his mother, got up to go to work, which although pleasant demanded a great effort since it had to be on a television channel daily to provide the latest information of the previous day and the first notes offered every day for the old continent.

That dawn between the rush and having to be impeccable to get on the air, he did not realize anything else but his safety when leaving the neighborhood where he lived, which by the way was not at all peaceful. His self-sacrificing mother accompanied him religiously in this early morning ritual, whose steps were perfectly synchronized.

Rodolfo loomed his face several times in the exit gate, and when he didn't see anything suspicious quickly with a fast sign he indicated to his mother to open the gate to take out his vehicle at the same time that he was embarking as a rally pilot, he would turn on the engine and leave quickly waiting only a few seconds until Doña Maria closed the heavy door garage, which offered security in that humble neighborhood.

The city at that time was fresh, calm, and to a certain extent, attractive because of the absence of traffic, which makes a city of 3 million inhabitants, a chaos in working hours. However, at the same time, in the darkest hours before dawn, the rest of the nightlife appeared, which in a large percentage of cases belongs to the underworld of the metropolis, full of drugs, danger and prostitution, but Rodolfo knew how to handle that line and with extreme caution he drove each morning with surgical precision, especially knowing the responsibility he had as a journalist with a super demanding public, which led him to establish himself an objective, which was never to miss his job, under any circumstances. And so much so that only once was on the verge of being absent due to a failure of his vehicle, but on that occasion ended the journey that remained on foot at that time of dawn and with the danger it represented for his personal safety, but continued with his record as he himself said, expanding his chest with pride. That was his goal and the reasonhe for his happinness.

"Horn sound (beep....beep...beep...beep...), that strange Cheito is always awake at this hour...(beep...beep...beep...) There must be a substitute and the relay fell asleep...Jesus Christ!! now who opens me'.

Rodolfo was a bit temperamental and perfectionist, he knew that this delay would bring problems to him during the video editing of the news.

Suddenly, "Good morning citizen," a man in uniform approached slowly in the gloom. He walked to the main entrance gate. Looking young, but nothing that resembled a guard, the individual spoke to Rodolfo.

"Citizen, do you work here?" Rodolfo fearfully replied that this was his daily check-in time. At that moment the uniformed man opened the gate manually and invited the now anguished Rodolfo, who at the time of advancing towards the parking lot of the Television Channel, realized that the individual was a military man.

"Rodolfo thought, "I'm sure they're doing some kind of electoral simulation. But for a moment ...hold on...son will not be elections", thought. At that moment Rodolfo tried to tell the uniformed that if there was a drill he could go away, that there was no problem.   To which the soldier pronounced a deep, firm and guttural, "Negative Lord, park and go to your place of work.

As he got out of the car, Rodolfo was approached by the same uniformed campaign soldier and he asked him, "Sir, you don't know anything? and obviously Rodolfo's face was a poem. "No, the chain didn't tell me anything about this simulation. The military man looked at the other comrades and said, "This is not a drill, it's a coup d'état.

With his face dislocated and stunned, he saw several of the soldiers who were in the semi-darkness and walked directly to the Hall main entrance. At that moment he noticed the absence of the usual guards and remembered Cheito, "My God where he will be, what will they have done to him". He tried to assimilate that picture, because between the hour of dawn, the surprise and the fear, he could not think, it was like in automatic, and he should finally arrive to the office of the morning program.

Surprised he dropped into the chair in front of the desk when suddenly Ring....ring...ring...the phone rang with a heartbreaking ring. The fright was so great that it almost stuck to the ceiling, clinging to the chandelier.

"Hello who call?." answered Rodolfo muttering. "It's me Rodolfo, the Economist Antonio Pedrique, tell me everything", he asked directly knowing that Rodolfo was going to be discovered talking at any moment.

At this momento the soldiers who were guarding the Television channel, the first thing they did was take the Communication center, so they were confident in having controlled all the communications, but it turns out that the office of the Morning Program had always had a direct line to receive calls, because at the time the program was on the air, there was no staff at the central. This gave the opportunity to establish communication from inside the channel to the street.

"Rodolfo, you must remain calm, everything will be fine, but you need to tell me how the military are dressed, if they have any emblem or anything that stands out to know if they are from the government or are coup plotters. Rodolfo thought as if trying to review what he had seen earlier, and suddenly said: "An strip....a tricolor band on the left arm. Every one have a band on the left arm with the flag".

 In that momento only it heard the economist mumble,

"Shut, it's the coup plotters." "The important thing is to remain calm because as hostages you can be used them to get out of this mess, and if you...... "Antonio I should cut off, I am listening steps....I can't talk".

(Sound of door opening) "Citizen where I can see this videotape". It was the same soldier who had approached him before and Rodolfo trembling with fright, with his technical experience at audiovisual level, took the small video cassette in his hand and observed him strangely and said to the soldier, "Wow this type of format is not on the channel. Here we work with the U-matic format, and all our equipments are unified with that platform for creating the network. However, normally the engineer Reinaldo arrives at 5 o'clock and he will give you better information. If you want to wait you can ask to him about.

After a long time, at dawn all the workers who had been captured were taken out of the canal and taken to the adjacent building, where the Ecclesiastical Residence of the Director and Founder of the Canal was located. At that moment when they were being moved, Rodolfo felt the need to run for safety, when at that moment one of the soldiers hit him on the head with the weapon, falling to the ground and immediately bathed in blood, by the cut caused by the stock of the gun. At the same time the women in the group, secretaries who had begun to arrive at the Television Plant, began to scream in panic. This attitude produced greater fear among the soldiers, who were already tense like a violin string, because the rumor was that the seizure of the capital had failed and what awaited them was difficult, they would even face jail.

In the same enclosure where the Ecclesiastical Residence was, there was a primary school, obviously empty due to the information that already flooded the screens of the regional and national Channels, not to mention the international ones. There, at the site, everyone exchanged ideas to try to decipher what was happening, while listening to the arrival of the Government's F-16 planes that began to fly across the sky over the television plant, which until now had continued to be under the control of the coup plotters.

An hour later in the Capital of the Republic the major coup plotter was handed over who in an adventure, more driven from the outside, by leftist doctrines, than by any other fact, was manipulated in a crude manner. This fact caused the group that took over the installations of the Television Channel, which had already taken over the Official Residence of the Regional Government, to hand itself over not before having negotiated with the necessary guarantees to be able to get out of the problem with the least amount of charges to face. The operation had been a colossal failure, leaving in the atmosphere that the situation would not stop there and that the South American country from that moment on would not be the same.

Chapter 2
Calm waters, brave people

1967

"Captain there is very bad weather the crew does not dare to leave in these conditions, the trip is extensive and the first hours in cases of long journeys should be less complicated", whispering, for not create anxious, the First Officer asked the Captain to postpone the departure for a few hours, but that did not proceed because in the coasts of South America were risking their lives, a significant number of guerrillas who from the Sierra in South America, had come down to the coasts to receive them and guide them into the mountains.

"Look, you are the first in command by my decision, if at any time again to mention that we postpone the departure due to bad weather, you will be arrested for eight weeks," replied the captain in a haughty tone like showing his dominion, and is that despite the nerves that existed, for being such a risky mission, he should must show firmness with the crew.

It was true that the weather was demoniacal, it was the month of April and despite the weather conditions, there was a strong storm in the Caribbean Sea, it was already hurricane season, so it was announced storm from the Florida península, until the Venezuelan area, unfortunately for the crew.

It was April 20, 1967 and in the heart of the Caribbean Sea was the crew whose only companion was the storm that lashed them. The personnel of both ships could not stick an eye for several days due to the ravages of bad weather. One of the boats was fatigued in its structure, so the second had to navigate side by side to avoid a tragedy that could have cost the lives of the members of that suicide mission. They saw land immediately and decided to reach the coasts to correct the problems with the ships. They were the coasts of the Dominican Republic. There they were taken advantage of and provided with more supplies and drinking water. At dawn, the bad weather continued, but even so they decided to set sail even against the warning for the boats, since the weather had to improve slightly.

After several days of travel and having overcome the onslaught of the weather, the situation improved for the mission headed for South America. The group made up of 12 crew members, 4 of island origin and 8 South Americans, wondered if it would have been worth embarking on such a difficult mission. The first question was what would be the Supreme Commander's interest in having sent them on such a long trip with weapons to train the young South American guerrillas. And above all, why couldn't it wait, why should the arrival on that date be so precise?

So many unknowns kept the crew busy figuring out any number of hypotheses, and although each of those present was there for their own personal decision, sometimes they did not cease to feel doubts as to the destiny they had chosen when forming part of the island's militias.

"Captain we are approaching the coast, but at this time we can not disembark, we must wait for the fall of the night to be able to do it without attracting attention," were the words of the First Officer, to which the Captain replied, "It is true, we must go ashore unnoticed, let's stop here, throw anchors and will wait for the night.

While everyone on the island was waiting for news about the mission, the group continued with the plan following each step with milimetrical precision.

"Commander, according to our calculations, the vessels must be about to reach land. In a few days they will have reached the first phase of our training plan for the young rebels who are in the coastal mountains of South America," said with a tone of satisfaction the aide looking at the Commander, who sat in his room with Habano in hand, staring at the horizon, imagining how the operation was going.
"Yes Jorge, if this goes wrong, there could be problems, because 5 years ago we failed in a first attempt of incursión. I trust that everything will go in a good way because if this work, we will celebrate 'Grande' ", and giving a deep breath to his tobacco, he let out a sigh that left the air cloudy for a few seconds.

On the other side, in the middle of the Caribbean Sea, it was about to materialize what would be the most risky incursion that any guerrilla troop has ever made in the annals of American history, sailing 1,115 nautical miles through the Caribbean Sea, obviously with several scales and even when the incursion was aimed at training rebel troops, then if it turned out, then they could devise a deeper and more complete plan.

"Lift anchors," shouted the Captain who was in the First ship, with which the second ship also reacted. In the middle of the night, the pressure of sailing blindly with headlights and lamps off, to leave no visual trace of their approach to land, both crews overlooked the fact that one of the vessels had a fatigued structure. Having land in sight they did not think the boat could be a problem.

By rowing and trying not to be detected, both ships began their approach guided only by the moonlight. The sea was chopped into the coast, that in a way favored the intention of not being spotted. What the intruders didn't know was that the area they were in was full of hidden reefs beneath the surface and with the sea calm the night before they didn't see anything strange. Suddenly a wave of great proportion, moved one of the ships and then in the vacuum left by it, was exposed a reef on which fell the boat, whose structure was felt, then the crew fell into the water and the ship was virtually submerged in part destroyed by the impact.

Immediately desperate cries were heard. Everyone knew that anyone who had fallen on the reefs would not live to tell the tale. Since the storm they had just started, they decided that the ship that had fatigued their structure would only have five crew members. Whit less weight their performance was going to be better. As this was the ship that ran aground, 5 crew members fell into the water. The most experienced sailors had fallen on the reefs.

"Orlando where are you? ....Ernesto! ....Ernesto! ....", they shouted from the first boat where the Captain was who was making enormous efforts to keep the rudder orienting the boat far from the reefs.

 "Captain we don't see them, we must rescue them", shouted the First Officer in the middle of the deafening beating of the furious waves on the hull of the ship, as if an unknown force was protecting the coasts of that noble country to which they wanted to dabble.

Suddenly 3 of the 5 crew members, taking forces from the deepest part, began to swim towards the boat, whose course had been controlled by Captain Raul, experienced in the naval arts and with high level studies in Marine Sciences.

"Here...here...", they shouted from the boat trying to orient their companions. They finally got to the boat and saved their lives. But two companions were missing. In a turn of the boat, Jose Antonio, another of the crew, spotted the fourth man and began to shout giving orientation to his companion, when they approached realized that it brought the fifth companion passed out fallen in disgrace, and were quickly assisted to climb into the boat.

Manuel was unconscious. He had hit his head with a reef. He was not breathing so they tried to reanimate him and gave him first aid with desperation, rotating between all of them, trying to recover the calm, while two were assisting Manuel, the others were panting with fatigue because of the tremendous effort they had made to get to the ship. Finally after 15 minutes they gave up their attempt. Manuel had died.

At this point the pressure that the members of the mission had exploded and they began to blame each other. At times the objective of the crossing was forgotten, until the Captain with a shout made them come back.

"We must reach land, it will soon dawn and we have just enough time for our meeting. Then we will take care of burying Manuel", said the Captain and with a turn of the rudder they bordered the reefs, to arrive at land just before the sun rose, they arrived with the precise time to bury Manuel at a certain distance from the beach.

The incident that the guerrilla group had before their disembarkation just before sunrise, made them make a serious mistake and this was to leave the ship without hiding it properly, because they would have been seen on the shore of the beach. However, the fact of not having hidden the ships caused, an hour later that a fisherman carrying out his work in the area, saw the 2 unknown boats, one destroyed by the reefs just on the shores of the beach, and the other at the edge of the bushes. When he saw the suspicious ships, especially the one that was almost shipwrecked, he wasted no time and reported it to the town authorities.

On the Island they presumed that everything was in order and according to the plan, since there were no reasons under normal conditions to think otherwise.

"Jorge, is there some information about Captain Raul and the mission in South America?",... "Not my Commander, but rest assured that the group sent is of high level"...said yes the assitant. "Please make me a report as soon as you have news",... "Yes Commander", was the sudden response of the aide Jorge.
After the disembarkation and with a sensitive casualty, since the quantity of elements for the mission was minimal, they distributed the load of weapons that they brought for the military training. As was to be expected, the road from the Coast to the Sierra was

going to be difficult, not only because of the twisted route, but also because of the load of arms and ammunition. This led to the establishment of an advance plan. This was based on the rotation of men loading the weapons, also making stops every 2 hours. Obviously at this rate it was going to be difficult to reach the Sierra in at least a few hours.

When the group was about to get inside a dangerous area forested, a contingent of 250 military personnel belonging to the Army of the Republic and the National Guard confronted the invaders. A battle began and lasted all night, as a result of the quantity and type of armament possessed by the invaders, as well as the amount of ammunition they had. The result of the confrontation was the casualty of 8 members of the mission, 2 detainees, an evaded invader and 1 deceased in the incident where he drowned.

Thirty-six hours took the authorities to locate the group of invading guerrillas, whose primary mission was to train the young rebel troops housed in the Sierra Andina of the South American Coast. In addition, the group brought a lot of arms as a concession, which the Island was handing to the commander of the group to begin training. Among the lot of weapons were AK47 which according to their serials had been sold by the Rep. Eska and the buyer had been the Caribbean island.

"Jorge was very discreet and waited for the best moment to give the message.

"Dime Jorge", (Tell me Jorge)...said the leader of the revolution.

"They caught 2 members of the Mission that we sent to the South American Sierra, the rest are dead. Only Alejandro was able to escape and is with the local guerrilla", to which the Commander responded,

"If we could not do it that way... we'll do it in the other way... Jorge give me a cigar, please..."

The attempted invasion of the island had not remained so. The government of the South American country offered a press conference to national and international media, introducing the two captured guerrillas from the island, who were forced to read aloud to verify their accent. In addition, the AK-47 rifles that were recovered by the government were presented, whose serials revealed that they came from the Eska Republic, and the date on which they were bought was also offered.

With these irrefutable proofs the next step was to make the complaint to the leading organism of the American continent. When the latter demanded explanations from the Island, its representants denied absolutely everything that had happened, alleging that the weapons had been stolen from their artillery park. From then on, the South American nation ratified the rupture of all diplomatic ties, which had been in force since 1961, due to a previous aggression by the Commander and the Government that forcibly obtained power in the Caribbean Island.

In the decade of the '60s were countless atrocities on the island, even when in 1959, without invitation the commander traveled with a commission to the International Airport of the Capital, violating diplomatic rules and presenting himself to the country completely armed. Politician and strategist Roberto Romancourt confronted this and demanded in his face the action he was carrying out. In that visit the Commander had 2 purposes, to look for Oil and to establish the Communism, seen the recent exit of the power of a Dictatorship of right. At that moment the living forces of the nation gave a negative to both requests, expelling the retinue that had broken into continental soil.
From then on, the Commander swore them.

Chapter 3
Breeding ground

After almost losing his life, Rodolfo dedicated himself to know a little more about why a group of soldiers had broken into the political scene in this way, which anyone would have thought was because of the precarious situation of the country, or perhaps because of the enormous corruption that existed at the time in all levels of government, be it national or regional, outside of one party or another. This was, in a way, the justification that was at hand to decipher the enigma into which the South American nation was entering.

However, as a result of his youth and inexperience, Rodolfo Vega, a young man of simple class, who, trying to overcome his economic limitations, dared to join the Armed Forces, could not understand the justification at hand. He was not satisfied with the argument of the economic situation.

Sportsman by nature, Rodolfo Vega after requesting to leave of the Armed Forces for not finding vocation of military service, began university studies, selecting the career of Journalist, same developed by his father and uncle, but also by his maternal grandfather, who lived days of dictatorship in his young years, back in 1950. Rodolfo always remembered a story that the family told about his grandfather, who, by the way, had the same name, and was one of the people who during the Dictatorship unfurled pamphlets and communication flyers to organize the groups that would eventually overthrow the regime of the moment.

That occasion that Rodolfo always remembered was when State Security arrived at his grandfather's house and began a requisition to try to find weapons. They literally tore up the house, raised tiles, even dug into the sand, looking for any weapon. After a good period of review nothing was found, just because grandmother had hidden a Smith & Wesson 38 caliber, under the fathoms and ashes of the stove.

Perhaps the journalistic sense of smell is inherited, but anyway it is inherited or not, the desire he always had to do journalism led him down the path of preparation and success. From childhood he accompanied his dad Don Roberto Vega, to different journalistic events, especially at the sports level, and that factor was decisive to make germinate that internal passion that only those who are born for Journalists feel.

Just in the middle of his university career he began to work always in the field of Journalism, his first article was written for the media in his School of Journalism. Always he was writing, reading, studying, learning languages, the more he do, the more he wanted, it was a kind of addiction.

In spite of his origin, speaking in economic terms he never had complexes because of the economic differences with his classmates or work colleagues, because his intelligent and loving mother since Rodolfo was a child told him, "Son, poverty is in the heart of people, it is not an economic condition. We may have economic limitations, but we have never been poor, on the contrary we have been blessed by God with moral, love and power mind", and with those concepts Rodolfo grew up and trained as a professional, as one of so many young people in the South American country.

Rodolfo always remembered clearly how just beginning to work, still in the midst of his difficult studies, he was able to make a credit to buy a car, with only 2 years of use. He was able to repair his mother's house and so many things, all with so many economic limitations. Then why that explosion of the group of soldiers who tried to overthrow the legitimately constituted government. And he wondered why if he, a simple mortal with work and studies which were absolutely free, had been able to progress. Sometimes he was asked as a journalist, and sometimes he was asked as a soldier, using that malicious instinct that develops in those military tasks.

That fixation left him neither sun nor shadow.... Something was behind, there was something that he could not understand... For now.

1974

Presidential Palace. The President of the South American Nation for that year received the Commander of the Island in the Main Hall, designed to receive the most important dignitaries. Cup of Cognac in one hand and Habano of the finest selection in the other. In this way the frozen relations between both nations are resumed since the month of June 1961, product of the contrary ideologies and the attempt of invasion that could never be punished, since the aggressor for 5 years no longer formed part of the Organization that gathers all the countries of the continent.

The decade of the '70s was great for the South American Republic. With stable oil prices, and taking advantage of this pacification, the guerrilla groups that were active in the Sierra decided to integrate into society by creating and strengthening political parties in order to be able to opt for power.

The country was at its best moment of cultural and economic development, the latter sector being divided into three strata. Primary, Secondary and Tertiary sectors. The primary sector employed 20% of the active population, the secondary sector 28%, and the tertiary sector 52%. That is to say, the unemployment rate was around 9 percent, really low, for what was coming.

The Decade of the '80s began with the impetus that it brought from the previous decade, only that it had a special characteristic and this was the corruption that began to take shape within the central government, and that was contaminating all government agencies. It's appropriate to point out that the media, according to their political bias, revealed the abuses committed by political representatives opposed to their interests. This social variable was one of the factors that may have provoked greater unrest and indignation among the population, because the sovereign knew about corruption at government levels and therefore knew that the selection of characters to lead the country had been erroneous. Two administrations of government that were from 1979 to 1989 destroyed what had been achieved in the decade of the "70s.

With the abrupt fall in oil prices, a fundamental source of income, and it could be said that approximately 80 percent of income came from the oil industry, the economy began to contract, and in 1983 the first great devaluation of the currency took place, which was accompanied by a tight exchange control, due to the flight of foreign currency, which was located by the order of 10 billion of the currency for the time. This scenario did not look good in a country in which the common people were accustomed to live comfortably.

1987

"Dad, I want to go to the Military School, since you don't want me to be a Journalist, the only option I see is to pursue a military career, specifically in the School of Officers of the Armed Forces, here is the registration brochure", were Rodolfo's harsh words to Don Roberto, who was visiting Rodolfo and Doña Maria's house, understanding that Rodolfo's parents had been separated for some years.

"Rodolfo is a surprise. I didn't expect this, I'd rather you studied for a lawyer or a doctor, but if it's your decision I'll agree, because I as a journalist I can tell you that I want something better for you, than to study journalism," Don Roberto told Rodolfo staring at him, as if in some way looking for the idea to be just a whim, but certainly Rodolfo was telling him the truth, he was about to begin his physical and mental exams to access the elite of young people who enlist in one of the best military academies in Latin America, at least he was for the time.

"Aspirant Cadet Vega Gonzalez, has been assigned to the first bedroom, ninth piece to the right. Here are your belongings and present yourself to Ensign Viana Atino for his reception," were the words of the commander of the Cadet Corps of the School of Officers, same for each of the members of the 1987 class.

At the age of 17, there is a lot that can be missed from home, especially having grown up with Fathers over protectors, as in the case of Rodolfo. However, this experience would form him for the rest of his life. Even from the very first day, when he queued up to go to the barbershop to cut himself flush, which was obviously the obligation, Rodolfo gradually realized that as they went in and out companions, they were leaving them a little more hair.

At this point he was moving slowly to roll little by little until the end of the line, he was retreating imperceptibly, and when he came to see, he was practically in the group of the last three. What would be his surprise when a Captain approached the Barber and asked him to speed up that it was time for dinner. Then the last 3 aspirants to Cadet, were victims of the sharp Double Blades !!

Three o'clock in the morning, and to the compass of the bull's-eye, all the Cadets jumped from the bed, to form themselves in front of each piece, in a position of firm sight and to the front, waiting for the instructions of the Ensign Major who, as usual, was assigned to the first bedroom. Once they were all formed, they went to the central park of the Academy for the first speech for the new members of the School, a course called propaedeutic or preparatory.

"All of us will go in double line formation to the training course or trot. No one can lag behind, no one can stop. These are the rules", said the commander of the platoon and in this way the 10-kilometer training began, which in principle would serve to break the cadet aspirants with less physical preparation, and filter the group until it was taken to a reduced number but with conditions and vocation for military life.

The temperature was 10 degrees centigrade, and while the officers, Alférez, and cadets belonging to the school, were wearing sports suits appropriate to the temperature, the "Rookies" only wore white shorts, white t-shirts and sports shoes.

"One...one...one, two, three...One...one...one, two, three....In the northern war, in the northern war, the battle is won like this, Aviation, leaves first...aviation leaves first...the Navy goes after...the Navy goes after...Soldiers go after three...soldiers go after trees...and we go too...and we go too..... One...one...one, two, three...", in that way Rodolfo began his physical preparation, which would be complemented with military preparation, closed order, in addition to the university level studies that were given to all cadets.

The preparation in the Military School of the South American country, was compared with the preparation of the West Point Academy of North America, in fact several of Rodolfo's companions were North Americans, carrying out exchanges of military studies, just as there were students from the Dominican Republic and so many other countries of America.

While the cadets developed their activities, the people in the street, the common citizen began to notice how the situation worsened. Inflation began to escalate and prices began to rise. Some companies that barely knew the honey of the bonanza began to feel the pressure of the economic situation, some even decided to close due to the imbalance in the market.

All this imbalance was caused by the fall in the prices of oil, the only sustenance of Venezuela, which until then had been known as the Saudi of the Americas. The popular class, with the passing of the months began to see their budget hit and week by week, month by month, the population was heating up. In 1978 there were presidential elections, and the winner Juan Guerrera, during his five-year term could not handle the storm, and with only one year of administration left to his five-year term, there was not much he could do. Without taking into account the levels of corruption that existed, especially in his administration.

While this was happening in the streets of every city in the South American country; inside the Military Schools, especially in the Academy, there were situations never seen in the annals of the country's military history.

The School of Officers and the Military Academy are united by an immense central square, and in spite of having a marked rivalry to demonstrate which of the two is better, exist a kind of brotherhood when it comes to decision making. In the corridors of both precincts some years ago the word had spread that things were changing from within, that there was a group led by a "Captain", that was changing the bases of the institutions. In fact, as a student of the Academy back in 1973, it was rumored that he had been punished for severe misconduct by handing out several flyers and pamphlets discreetly promoting 'Socialism'.

This was considered a serious offense typified in the regulations, by the fact of the oath taken when initiating Studies in the Schools, since one of the requirements to be able to enter was not to belong to any political party, in other words it was demanded to be "apolitical", for being able to be a Cadet. Were also known stories in which, being a lover of oratory, in some official acts of the Military Academy, he let escape some phrase of double sense, always around the same subject.

Rodolfo, with that innate touch of Journalism, continued to investigate and knew that several Generals had set up files for him to be expelled from the military compound, and on the first occasion one laboriously structured file with irrefutable evidence of the indoctrination he was carrying out, with his fellow students, disappeared as if by magic, when the General in charge left it on the desk of the Director of the Academy.

This situation alerted and suggested that the Captain in question was not alone, and was better sponsored than many believed. As an additional piece of information, it was known that the second time the Captain had his expulsion file created; when it was presented by the General who had carried out the investigation and was delivered into the hands of the Director, the Director took it and in front of the General, placed it in the trash can. It was too late the effect of left indoctrination was entrenched at least among some Officers of the Military Academy.

During a sentinel night, the aspirant to Cadet Vega Gonzalez, had a mixfeelings in the mind and he felt the need to speak, ask questions and ask for advice.

"My Brigadier, permission to speak with you," Rodolfo asked his companion on duty that night, with the intention of clarifying some doubts about the Captain's subject. "Tell me, Vega Gonzalez, what's wrong with you, you feel nostalgia, you miss your family? because that's perfectly normal", in that way the Brigadier broke a little the protocol of military respect.

"Yes my Brigadier, i'm little nostalgic and wanted to know if I could talk to you about it. I wanted to know if you felt this and how you'd gotten over it," Rodolfo said directly, as his guardmate snorted a puff of cigarettes, at the time he offered one.

"No thanks My Brigadier, I want to be in shape for the baseball tournament that starts soon," ...Vega replied.

"Of course you're one of the pitchers.....Well Vega I want to be honest, you are very multifaceted, and is very appreciated in the School for Baseball, and also belongs to the music group, but to be here, to devote your whole life to this is necessary to have a vocation, and that sometimes is discovered being here. Now I ask you; do you have a vocation to be a soldier?", the Brigadier dropped that direct ball.

"The truth my Brigadier, I am not sure", answered Rodolfo.

The Brigadier went further and told him that things were changing in a certain way in the Institution, and that this change was going to be dangerous, even with civilians. These are changes that the country needs to take another direction. The Brigadier gave him an example, to see how far his subaltern would go.

"Imagine that at this moment your parents are approaching to the Military School carrying weapons and bombs to attack the headquarters and destroy it. There was a sepulchral silence as if time had stood still. Then Rodolfo anxiously replied, "I would stop them and approach them and convince them to change their mind"....The Brigadier told Rodolfo, "You know that Vega, I recommend that you ask for the leave, because your answer should have been to shoot until you annihilate the target, even if in this case that target is your parents.

That advice was a kind of "click". From that moment Rodolfo saw the things in a different way, that conversation had been very helpful and understood that this was not his vocation, but he also took different things on the air and he put it together and understood that something was moving that was not seen and perhaps did not understand well by his scarce 17 years and little experience in life.

If Rodolfo ever asked to be discharged, because he considered that he was not prepared for that world, he first had to show that despite his young age he could obtain the dagger granted in the first year and that he would be certified as a Cadet of the South American Republic, so he took his stay to learn more about what was happening under the floor of the Institution and above all he wanted to decipher the stories of the Misterious "Captain".

"I told you to stop," shouted a second-year cadet from a distance to Rodolfo, who was stand held in front of the soft drink dispenser. The aspiring cadets were forbidden to consume candy at the wrong time, and Rodolfo who had stopped in front of one of these machines, nervously waiting until the can of soda came out, literally flew with the can in his hand.

Running through all the corridors and slipping at each crossroads avoiding their pursuer, as they found themselves with work shoes ready to enter classes. For a moment Rodolfo thought he had escaped because he slipped away and entered his classroom without being seen, but his persecutor entered all the classrooms looking for his victim, until by his hectic breathing he found him and told:

"Look at me, if I talk to you, you fly towards me, not in the opposite direction. Now as a punishment you will present this can of soda to me every time I ask for it," told the second year cadet and after he signed the aluminum can with a key, so in this way there was no escape. Rodolfo could not drink the soda; and what a worse punishment for a young cadet in full preparation phase, when the demand for glucose is so high. A week later Rodolfo open the can and drank it, assuming what it represented. Fortunately there was no problems with this ever.

Rodolfo was still curious about that Captain who admired Socialism, until a group conversation of second year cadets with greater ease and confidence for the rank achieved, one of the members told a story that allowed those present to understand a little more about what it was, They said that in the Captain's family there were left-wing political activists, and that the Captain's entrance to the Academy was planned even though the captain's intellectual level was not high, he had a great use of the word. But the only way to open the Academy doors was through sport, since once inside with the charisma he had it would be easy to get positions, and so it was.

The Captain's Dad, has been a politician, one of the "good ones", because he had gone through all the political parties of the Republic, from those on the right to those on the left, as most of the country's politicians have done, they are accommodated where they get the best dividends.

"Armando, but I learned that the Captain a few months ago created a closed group, ie as a club of friends or something like that," Rodolfo asked one of his colleagues with some fear because that point was a taboo subject. But as they were among quite relaxed friends, those who knew the subject looked around and as if saying to themselves, well, if the group is trying to grow we should open up a bit.

"Indeed," replied Armando, "The Captain has been forming a Movement for some years now, only that it can no longer be kept totally secret, it has grown a lot. The Group calls MBR2000, that is to say Revolutionary Bolivarian Movement 2000, whose purpose was to participate in the events in the country. My dad, who is a driver for the public transport, has told me on countless occasions that it is impossible to live like this, that money is no longer enough for anything because corruption has produce a hole in our pockets.

Armando continued, "The theme of every day on the routes that my father makes is the same, the people are dissatisfied, the people are angry, because while the people are in need, the politicians keep drinking whiskey in the bars of restaurants, with the people's money, and in this government of Juan Guerrera it is worse. Imagine that my Dad says that he can barely afford to buy diablitos, cheez Whiz, grains, caraotas, and fourth-rate meat, it really difficult to live in this way.

Armando explained more or less how was the life of his Pope, a typical inhabitant of the Capital of the South American Republic. And he emphasized, because many of his companions, if not all of them, were from the interior and 2 were from the Dominican Republic, who were in the School by exchange of Academies.

"Then my 'Captain' is fed up with it, because he carried it a lot when he was little", Armando emphasized, and at that moment Rodolfo could not keep quiet and commented: "You knew that the Captain was about to be expelled twice when he was a student".

"And as you know that", Jesus answered, a little older than the rest, and of 2nd year and and a second year rank, who until now had remained silent.

"Well, inquiring and asking, because if I am here I must know where I am standing. They caught him handing out leaflets with left-wing ideas, socialist slogans like those you read and see in universities".

Roberto jumped quickly, "Fuck look at at the new one, he came out investigator, come here, do 50 chest push-ups, but now!, by the way. And don't repeat that again, did you hear me?", ordered Roberto looking at Rodolfo.

"Yes, my cadet," answered Vega, between flexion and flexion.

As a result of that meeting Rodolfo had with his platoon mates, he began to tie up loose ends, and knew that something being structured. Those who did not know anything, did not perceive anything, but those who knew the captain, were aware of everything, especially when in a conversation someone arrived and quickly became silent, that group belonged to the captain's lodge.

Rodolfo anxiously waited daily for the hours of meeting with his squad and platoon companions, whether in closed-order practices, in which Rodolfo was a true champion by the way, or in sports practices, music group rehearsals, and the Military Arts and Sciences Classes. Those were the moments in which day by day he was learning what was being organized in the shadows.

Chapter 4

The plan

After three long months doing the course of entrance or propaedeutic period, finally the moment arrived so awaited. The act of delivery of the 'Dagger', and the first ascent, from Aspirant to Cadet, to Cadet of the South American Republic.

Relatives and friends of the 240 "Rookies", as the newcomers are known, attended the event. It is a term that is used in a derogatory tone, but that does not bother this legion of young people at all, since they are the cream of every generation in the country.

"I'm happy to have achieved this goal, but the greatest will be the one I'm going to get this weekend," shouted Rodolfo to his classmates, but the comment was not exclusive to him, everyone wanted to have a few drinks after so long without alcohol. In words more, or words less, it was the feeling of all those boys that in that moment began a new stage of their lives.

"Rodolfo...Rodolfo"! someone shouted at him and when he turned around it was Don Roberto with Doña Maria, who were traveled from the province to see the unforgettable act.

"Dad, Mom! God! what a joy, I could not see them before the act, that is like a kind of tradition, nobody can see their friends or relatives before the reception of the 'Dagger'. How are you?", and they fused into a hug, which was full of joy and pride, especially because of Rodolfo's young age, in this case that had more recognition.

"Dad, when you both arrived, where are you both staying?" asked Rodolfo. Apparently his companions were going to have a party that he did not want to miss. "Well Roberto we are well, we arrived at the house of Elizabeth and Amilcar, who kindly allowed us to spend the weekend with them, but on Monday we should going back, remember that I have a lot of work and your Mom can not stay alone in the capital," replied Don Roberto, who despite being separated from Doña Maria they built a perfect friendship.

"I have an idea, I meet the boys, I sneak out as soon as possible and then we can go out to eat and share on Sunday, visiting different places, what do you think," said Rodolfo. Don Roberto nodded gladly because he was really exhausted, and a break would do them good.

"Enjoy son you deserve this and again we are very happy with this goal that you have achieved," and with a hug they said goodbye, not without first releasing a couple of tears of emotion and pride.

That Sunday was special for Rodolfo, he was three months without see his parents, and that was not usual. He lived with his mother and saw his father at least once every 15 days. That's why the moments were emotional. Rodolfo the first thing he told his parents was that he could not go around certain sectors, not only because of their dangerousness, but also because they were suspicious of the Cadets, and they could steal the Dagger, an emblematic element that they had to protect at all costs. That's why the best thing they did was to go to an Eastern Shopping Center, and there they had lunch, ate ice cream, walked, and then saw a film of Agent 007, it was the premiere of 'Octopus', with Roger Moore, and Rodolfo died for this type of films.

As night fell, Rodolfo told them that they had to return because the time of their entry was approaching and that point was sacred, any delay could cost him his next night, and that possibility was not on the table.

"Dad, thanks you for coming to this importan moment, Mom, I'm going to miss you," and at that moment Doña María burst into tears, but immediately she held back so as not to spread her evident sadness in the air. "My son, may God protect you and keep you away from dangers, see you soon. Rodolfo, with a slight smile, told them, "I love you both very much," and slowly he walked down the hallway to the the School.

Once at the School, Rodolfo turned quickly and disguisedly over his shoulder to take a last look at his parents, but they were no longer within sight. After this weekend, in which at times he had his usual life, it seems that everything was going to be more difficult, however he did not want to leave without knowing what was happening, silently and slowly under the military platform of which he was already part.

"Sir Commander, I request permission for speaking Sir", with the respective military protocol Rodolfo asked to speak with his platoon commander, in the middle of a last shift night guard, which was being carried out in the Central Hall of the School.
"Yes Cadet you can continue," replied his superior.
"My Commander, I wanted to tell you that I have been listening to some of my classmates, for accident to talk about a little delicate subjects, but when I arrive they are silent as if hiding something,

and I would like to know what it is, because now I am part of this School and I need to feel integrated. I imagine what it's all about but I'd like to be sure." With this, Cadet Vega opened the consultation with his Commander, and perhaps the Pandora's box, but at the end of the day he was able to tell the story.

Commander Viana Atino was the commander of most important platoon in the School. That group of soldiers is to which by fate belong Cadet Rodolfo Vega. It is not by chance that things happen. The Platoon inhabits in the First Bedroom, the same one in front of the Central square, the same one that should be ready for any emergency contingency.

The one visited by the Presidents, Diplomats and Directors of all the Military Schools in the world. So it was a very cohesive group. After all and due to their personalities, Commander Viana Atino and Cadet Rodolfo, found a good relationship, and except for an small incident one morning while they were doing the morning exercises, when Cadet Rodolfo came up with the idea of move his Commander in the free race, they were fine. After that moment, the Cadet didn't feel like it anymore, because the 'punish' that they put him was not normal. However, now they had a friendly relationship, despite the difference in military rank.

"Vega, so you want to know more about it, you'd better stay calm, you're too cool to know anything about everything. Later on it will be another story", were the words of Viana Atino in a tone of advice for her subaltern. At that moment Rodolfo said: "That's means that here all my companions know more than the account". said the Cadet Rodolfo Vega in a somewhat haughty tone that did not leave room for comment, because it was the truth, very few, not to say the only one who did not know what was happening was him. In the atmosphere reigned for a few minutes the silence. "This good Cadet Vega from this moment has compromised his life. I'll tell you what it is. And lighting a cigarette, Ensign Viana Atino sat down to talk to the impetuous Cadet Rodolfo Vega.

Saturdays were very important to the cadets, but especially to the Ensigns who usually stayed overnight, that is, they could sleep outside the school grounds, while the cadets had to return at a certain time, but the next day they could go out again, if they had the permission. That was the rule, with a few exceptions.

Early in the morning they called the First Bedroom Commanders through the loudspeakers. That is, the Commander Major, and the

Auxiliaries Commanders. They were informed that there was a surprise visit by the Commander General of the Navy, and obviously that implied a visit to the First Bedroom. Immediately everything was transformed and tensed because the First Bedroom had to be impeccable, shiny, brilliant, and speaking in military terms, that meant that the pride of the School that was the First Bedroom, had to be 'perfect' because the inspection was going to be thorough.

A last check was carried out and everything was verified to be in order and extremely shiny, each member's shoes clean up to the sole, perfectly lined curtains, lights complete and aligned, clothes shelves completely arranged inside and well closed, beds absolutely stretched. And to be honest there was nothing new.
When the time came, everyone was placed in front of each room in the first bedroom. "Firm Attention", the Commander of the Cadet Corps let out with force. And at that moment, as arrogant and daring as he was, she put a white glove on her right hand to touch and make the corresponding tour during the Magazine. All the cadets, without exception, swallowed thick and closed their eyes as if praying to God that everything would be all right and that the Commander of the Cadet Corps would not exceed his arrogance with the Commander General of the Navy.

Everything was going marvelously, until the tour stopped at the Ninth right piece, right in the cubicle to which Cadet Rodolfo Vega belonged, with one Commander, a 2nd year Brigadier and a 3rd year Cadet. Right there the group of visitors entered, dialoguing boasting about the neatness of the "First Bedroom" and after walking the white glove through diverse areas like the bed, above and below, the sink, shoes, floor; The commander of the Corps of Cadets came up with the idea of passing the gloved hand over the wooden shelf that served the function of wardrobe, and tenuously there was an almost imperceptible spider's web.

Everything continued. They finished the tour and when everyone had left, the Commander of the Cadet Corps returned to the bedroom and said in a firm voice. "The Commanders of this dormitory do not have an overnight stay this weekend. After that there was an absolute destruction of the dorm staff, including Cadet Rodolfo Vega.

After a couple of weeks, things went back to normal. The Commanders in their overnight stay and the Cadets with their Saturdays and Sundays out. Rodolfo didn't know many people in the capital, so he went out to the house of some friends who were originally from the city where he had been born.

"Amilcar como te va, we had already several weeks without seeing each other," says Rodolfo while giving him a hug.

"Today hot dogs come out with chips," Amilcar replied with equal joy and telling him that they could also visit a couple of girl friends they were sure to like. Rodolfo told him that he wanted to talk to him for a while, that there was something important that he wanted to tell him and he couldn't wait.

Faced with Rodolfo's seriousness, he could not refuse and only asked for a few minutes to call his girl friends to apologize and tell them that they were not going to be able to leave that Saturday. At the same time I ask them if the next day they were without commitment that they were called to coordinate any outing to eat.

"Amilcar, brother. I think I'm in trouble", looking down Rodolfo pronounced these words that were tinged with a hint of nervousness.

"What did you do Rodolfo, look that I know you and I know how volatile you are. Tell me what happened so that you, so cheerful and jovial, would be like this", Amilcar whipped him so that he could tell him in detail what was happening.

Rodolfo began by telling him the details of those three long months he spent locked up in the School, physical details, studies, closed order, anecdotes. Then he told him about the night guards he used to do, and in which he learned to smoke. He also told him how he accidentally found out about the 'Capitan' and the movement that was created and finally told him about the conversation with Commander Viana Atino and everything he told him. In the middle of Rodolfo's summary of Amilcar, he suddenly realized that his Commander Viana Atino had threatened him with death.

"Shutt" but Viana Atino practically threatened me with death and I hadn't processed this until now", Rodolfo jumped ejected from his chair, because of the trance he was going through. Amilcar asked him, "Rodolfo, because you think that, I think you are creating extreme things. Nobody in their right mind is going to threaten someone just like that.

Inmmediately he went to the refrigerator and bring him a glass of fresh water, looking for a way to calm him down. Rodolfo was staring, as if scrutinizing in his memories any word or perhaps a gesture that would allow him to justify that he was wrong in his appreciation. But it was in vain. The more he remembered the moment of the conversation, the more he confirmed that he was in tremendous trouble.

It wasn't long after the conversation, when Rodolfo left Amilcar's apartment, extremely nervous and on the way to the School he passed the mental film of his conversation with Commander Viana Atino.

"Cadete Vega, I'm going to tell you everything so that you don't feel excluded, but in this way you are compromising your life", those words echoed in Rodolfo's mind. The Commander began his story: "Cadete Vega, the Captain, is the product of a plan that has been in the making for a long time. Originally the idea was that the brother of the Captain, who is much more intelligent, enter the Academy to develop the plan that has long been projected. But unfortunately it could not be achieved due to Alan's physical deficiencies. The Professor is a statesman, someone better prepared and more intelligent, but he was rejected in the entrance exams". Rodolfo had his five senses on his Superior officer listening to absolutely everything. Viana Atino continued his story.

"It was then that they turned to Lugo, the Professor's younger brother, and thought of him for several reasons. The main one was that Lugo was a sportsman and with great charisma, besides he had a great talent for oratory and leader's gift which made the idea attractive. The rest could be filled with reading. The books contain everything, especially those of Socialism", At that moment the Cadet Vega showed surprise and this alerted the Commander. The moment was filled with tension, but at that point everything was consummated, so Viana Atino continued.

"A few months ago, one of our cadets unfortunately died at the hands of the underworld because he had approached the areas of the capital prohibited by our school. Apparently he met a girl and she lived in one of the danger zones for us, but he did not pay attention and they took his life to assault him". It was regrettable, even more because a week ago he had asked to leave for family reasons." At this point Rodolfo was pulled from his thoughts. The taxi driver was asking him to pay him because they had arrived at the entrance gate to the school.

"Cadet's death ? .... what if it wasn't a robbery ? What if he wanted to go on leave and they didn't let him cause he knew too much?". Cadet Vega's head kept turning. He felt fear, anguish, anxiety, rage, he had to do something, because little by little he was diminishing his capacity of objective analysis, product of his fear and anxiety. "I know what I'm going to do, I just hope nothing happens before I leave school," he thought quietly and began to plot what he had in mind.

The first thing was to think about everything he had talked about with Commander Viana Atino in relation to that group that had been created and with which he had committed his life without knowing it. Then he thought about what Amilcar said: "Rodolfo I can't tell you what you should do, but I think you should sacrifice what you are doing and disappear. You have to find a way to disappear, because they can hurt you". And while he was having a kind of film about all the conversation with Commander and Amilcar, he realized that he was sweating profusely and also that his lips were dry, all this because of the nerves that were ravaging him.

In fact Amilcar's advice was very opportune because according to Rodolfo's intuition, he had been under surveillance for some days. He felt that someone was watching him before any movement he made. If he went to the casino, a group follow him, if he approached the quartermaster, he would also notice the same thing. It was such a feeling that he decided to be alone for as little time as possible, avoiding a possible attack on his person. He had become paranoid.

One of the things that reassured him a little, was that at no time did he tell anyone of his intention to ask for been disenrolled. That decision he made after speaking with the Brigadier in which he told him that he had to shoot to kill at that moment if his father or mother approached through the central courtyard of the School to attack the barracks. From that moment things changed for him and nothing was the same, he thought that the sacrifice he was making to be there to develop a career and with which to live, was not justified because his scale of values was totally different. In his order of priorities was first God, then his parents, then the family, and what military life offered, or at least what they wanted to instill in him was not what he expected.

Five o'clock in the morning, (Trumpet sound) !!!!!.....
All rookies should be ready in the Central square for the start of the daily trot. Usually before the trumpet sound, each Cadets under the savannah with a flashlight in mouth, began their preparation to not be late to the formation of the platoons.

Each one was endorsing the shorts and the white t-shirt, when previously they had cleaned the face and rinsed the mouth, only remaining pending to put on the sport shoes, to leave running to the site of formation.

"Attention Firmmmmm" .....This is your Commander Viana Atino Platoon".... and in this way the short morning speech began, and then in the darkness that precedes the dawn the group went out into the open field. That day an incident would occur wich was used by cadet Vega to perfection for his plan to get out of the mess.

"One...one...one, two, three...One...one...one, two, three...".
And so I begin the journey. With all the platoons orderly leaving towards the 'Tiger's hill', so called because of the difficulty that represents to raise it to the trot or walking. Every day in each exit to train the squads made competitions, to leave seated which of the squads was the fastest, the best prepared and therefore the leader squad, and always in the last stretch they were absorbed in a race of speed in which the representative of the squad that arrived first during the day, would deserve the respect of the rest. That day there was a more accentuated push than normal, and in a curve there were 3 squads in descent to an approximate height of 50 meters above the level of the plain.

At that moment, the Cadet Vega who averaged almost one meter 90 centimeters, with enormous strides received the approval of his Commander, and squeezing the step was able to get in front with the other platoons, until in a moment felt a blow in the upper part of his back. A kind of push. Vega then rolled downhill, spinning on his chest and then falling down the precipice whose bottom were some lush trees.

The rest of the cadets began to shout for help, and began the search for the wounded cadet, suddenly arriving a rescue helicopter with several paramedics, some of whom descended on the bushes. There was no trace of Cadet Vega. The Commanders of the three platoons were going crazy because the cadets of lower years were their responsibility. Besides, what justification were they going to give in relation to the competition of platoons. What a big Problem was created in the Military School.

After more than an hour one of the paramedics shouted that they had seen the bleeding body of Cadete Vega. When he approached he found that he was wounded but stable. They called the Helicopter and gave him the precise location, through a flare. Then a First Aid basket took the Cadet out of the ravine and transported him to the Military Hospital.

The diagnosis of the medical examination was mild cranial trauma, fracture of a rib on the right side, and displacement of a vertebra in the lumbar region, for which the cadet had rest for several weeks recovering from the wounds inflicted. It was never known who pushed him, it was never known who wanted to assassinate him. What was known was that some cadets realized that he wanted to request the disenrolled of the force.

During the following days, Cadet Vega, due to the gravity of the case was visited by the Deputy Director of the School, who was a very close friend of Cadet Vega's father, but until that momentthen was not known. At that moment Rodolfo took advantage of that link of which both made reference and asked the disenrolled. Rodolfo said that he no longer wished to continue in the School. This fact, added to the spinal injury suffered by the Cadet, was enough argument to dismiss him. In less than a week Rodolfo Vega, having delivered the Dagger of Cadet, had received his military leave and had left the country on an unknown course.

Chapter 5

Chain reaction

1988

Doña Maria and Don Roberto could not wait to see and hug Rodolfo, who a year ago had left for the United States with the argument of studying English, but in reality had been escaping from the situation he had to face during his stay at the Military School. However, the whole group swore not to mention that chapter in the life of the family anymore. Friends and acquaintances were simply told that the military career had ended as a result of Rodolfo's back injuries, from which he was, by the way, completely recovered. The displacement of the lumbar vertebra had been corrected and he was ready to embark on a new phase of his life.

"Through the corridor Rodolfo approached with a more mature aspect countenance and considerably heavier. "Son i have miss you so much", said his mother and in a long and deep embrace they remained in the middle of the corridor for a long time. They quickly left the airport, to go home, to rest because the trip from Los Angeles had been a bit overwhelmed, not counting the hours of difference, which of course alter the biological rhythm.

When Rodolfo arrived home he could not stand his anxiety and, as expected, immediately communicated to his father his irrevocable decision to study journalism, with or without his help, to which Don Roberto replied, "Son that's youre decision and any stumbling block or change of plans would be youre sole responsibility.
I'm not going to fight, because after all, everyone does what they think, but you can't count on me". Those words, so strong and deep, were assumed by Rodolfo in a mature way, like if their meaning were, 'yes I accept it'.

For him it was the first of many goals that he would accomplish during the course of his career.
As the School of Social Communication was his closest objective, he immediately processed everything to initiate a Degree in Communication Sciences, thereby giving free rein to his dreams contained in his DNA.

While this was happening with Rodolfo Vega's personal life, the South American country remained tense. Rumors, some protests and with some politicians who never lacked, throwing firewood to the fire. The elections of December 1988, would be a valve that the people were waiting to release so many pressures. At this time they preceded a pair of catastrophic presidential periods, in which there was a resounding devaluation and consequently exchange control, and in the other, rather or in the two five-year periods, an unprecedented corruption in the country. Inflation during the election year was at 35 percent, five points below the year '87. However, the situation maintained a climate of instability.

Everything suggested that the winner of the race would be CAP, Castor Arturo Penso, and in effect achieved the victory with which for the second time would be President of the South American Republic. CAP had defeated Gato Hernandez with 52 percent of the votes. and the people celebrated this victory because CAP in its first period had made a good management, obviously supported by the oil prices which at the time were at the maximum, because the Opep decided not to sell more oil to the countries that supported Israel in the Yom Kippur War, so the barrel went from costing 1 dollar and 62 cents, to worth 9 dollars and 31 cents, ie had a rise of 475 percent, and this CAP took advantage in his first management.

However, history was different on this occasion, since the fall in oil prices had provoked a price crisis in products and an excessive inflation, which was also seasoned by corruption, becoming a great social crisis. To top it all off, there was a character like 'Wolf' on the lookout, who was on the lookout for how the world was moving, and he continued with his intentions to put his hand on the South American Country, and that was none other than the Commander of the Caribbean Island.

"Viva Castor Arturo Penso.....que viva CAP", were the cheers that were heard rumbling in every corner of the South American country's geography. CAP was the salvation table of the people who, remembering their first mandate, celebrated in the streets with exaggerated joy. Young people in caravans, with music, in the bars of the Capital was a continuous celebration. Activities of any kind were carried out in honor of the man who in his first term guided the country with good hand, creating sources of employment, and nationalizing oil in 1976. CAP was also a very lucky man, at least until then.

An important point, worrying and on which the representatives of the national active life coincided, was the danger represented by the fact that CAP had achieved this victory using the 'populist' argument, the one used by the politicians offering everything to win the masses and then being unable to comply, either because the rest of the powers of the Government does not give him carte blanche, or simply because the economic resources available to a nation do not allow it. The latter one was to be the case for which CAP was sacrificed by the system of government of the Republic, and something more.

"My Colonel, flights 11457 and 11458 have arrived from the Island with the retinue of the President Commander of the Island. Both flights come with accompaniment of around 300 people", that was the message via radio transmitter emitted by the Director of Protocol of the Libertador Air Base, for Colonel Sebastian Fernandez, Director of the Base, and in charge of receiving the Presidents who had been invited to the inauguration of the recently elected President of the South American Republic that February 2.

"Director, but it is an exaggerated number of companions the one that brings the delegation of the Island", commented the Colonel worried, since they were not expecting such a big group. "See how it resolves, and do it quickly because that complicates the situation," said the Colonel.

This fact was going to be transcendental in the life of the nation. The Commander of the Island always did what he wanted, and also did it with an arrogance that altered the tranquility of any host. but this time they planned an accurate blow to the tranquility of national life in the South American Republic.

The exaggerated number of companions, that is to say 300 with the pretext that it was security personnel, was calculated with all the intention, since due to the ceremonial and protocol, and to the lack of time to process everything due to the surprise, the personnel of the Air Base, could not check the luggage of the 300 companions of the Commander, giving green light to the delegation so that it entered to national territory by a superior order and acelerate the entry and consequently not to make wait to the other delegations that were in queue in the zone of taxeo of the runway. The members of the Island knew that it was going to be that way, so they were able to introduce more than 300 weapons and ammunition in the luggage, whose objective was to make them reach the rebel forces that were organized in the Sierra Andina and would be the war material to be used in the first attempt of insurrection in the South American country, called the 'Carajazo'.

"One of the assistant had told the leader of the island that everything was in order and calm.

Since his arrival in power in 1959, after coming down from the Sierra Isleña, the Commander had wanted to expand his power and influence, speaking in terms of the Caribbean area, only that the lack of economic resources prevented it. This was the reason because from the beginning he became interested in oil and the wealth of the South American nation. In this sense there were no less than 7 attempts of invasion by force, with weapons, but he could never crystallize his objective.

For the Commander it was vital to merge his project with the richest country in the area, due that the Union of Communist Countries was gradually withdrawing the economic support it had provided until then. The only way to maintain its Communist expansion was by invading a rich country and the one at hand was the king of oil in the Caribbean.

On the morning of February 27, 1989, the spark of protest was ignited in a nation that had not experienced such episodes for a long time. According to the investigations, the attitude of the inhabitants of the Region of Arenas, where the story began, was spontaneous, but as the day progressed, the protests and looting expanded, it was thought that somehow the accelerator of that event was planned, taking into consideration that history revealed the entry into the country, only 25 days before, of an arsenal of weapons and ammunition that could well have been used to exacerbate the spirits and despair of the people.

"Come here, here, there is meat, help me to raise this beef, call them quckly Jorge and Wilker. Look for them fast pussy we are going to take this fast".
Pedro was an inhabitant of the city of Arenas, he was desperate because for days he did not take food to his house and his children did not eat complete for a long time. The same thing happened with the group of friends among whom they picked up and took half a beef, after forcibly opening a butcher's shop in the area. The story was continuous, it seemed like a horror movie at high speed. While Pedro and his group emerged victorious from

their attempt, another settler like Rafael was injured in the leg by a gunshot, as business owners were protecting their property and values. There were groups of people running some with kitchen utensils, others with clothes, with food. People were taking everything in their path.

The forces of law and order were trying to contain a kind of unleashed rage, a rage that was understandable, because they felt deceived by the newly elected CAP President.

"They were shouts of fear and were accompanied by a confused attitude, that happens when the irrational brain takes over the rational in the human being.

They were ten terrible days that lasted the 'Carajazo' and marked the life of the South American Nation. Nothing would ever be the same, something changed forever in the DNA of the population.

But what happened? That man was elected with 52 percent of the votes in the election! only 25 days ago? But he also had a previous administration that was supposed to be good, for whatever reason. That is why it is still thought that there were strange forces that accelerated that event, obviously in addition to other sociological factors that have to do with the populist argument that I use to win the elections.

During his electoral campaign, Castor Arturo Penso, known as CAP, offered social inclusion as a hook, using as a platform his first administration, and of course the springboard left by his two predecessors, who made terrible governments with mistakes, such as the devaluation of the currency, exchange control, and above all had been permissive with corruption, knowing that the people do not forgive this type of facts.

But he, Castor Arturo Penso once the victory was obtained, and as a recommendation of the International Organizations announced a list of measures that were completely opposed to those offered in his way to the Presidential chair, such as, for example, an increase in all the food items except in 14 which corresponded to the basic basket, a temporary increase in the credit rate, a progressive increase in public services, an increase in public transportation, a 30 percent increase in public sector salaries, among others.

But there were two lines in which an explosive mixture was created, because in one it was the pocket of the masses, of the sovereign, which was the increase in the price of gasoline by up to 100 percent. * And the second the most dangerous, which was the progressive elimination of import taxes and tariffs, which touched the pockets of the big businessmen of the South American nation. The economic experts wonder if the degree of social frustration and the unstable economic panorama of the country for the moment, were a real justification for what was experienced in the 'Carajazo'.

However that social explosion was marked as the beginning of the destruction of the South American Republic, caused by a combination of external factors.

However, despite the tragedy experienced by the inhabitants of the metropolitan area of the capital and the sector called Arenas, the establishment of the economic package was still in place, in fact and as planned in effect, on March 7. One day before the end of the protests, the price of food was suddenly raised. This fact was accompanied by another element that perhaps was what calmed the spirits, since the executive order was emitted for the realization of the first direct elections of Governors and Mayors, fact that until the moment did not exist.

'Meritocratically' from the central Power these positions were designated by finger, being this in many cases counterproductive, since in occasions they sent an oriental like Governor of the West and therefore. Perhaps this decision ended up appeasing the mood in the center of the country. But the beginning of the destruction had begun, not only because of the discontent of the population, but also because of external forces that pushed to overthrow the government and in this way change the democratic system that had been in force since the fall of the right-wing dictatorship overthrown in 1958.

"Rodolfo, I've seen that you don't feel very comfortable in the newspaper, what's going on, did you have a problem? tell me there's trust between us". Alice, one of Rodolfo's best friends, was worried because she saw him melancholic and dull. He responded by shaking his head from side to side, as if trying to check himself to see if there was anything out of place, but he said no. He said, "No, I don't know. Maybe it's lack of affection," said Rodolfo laughing, because Alice was a very pretty woman and between the two there was a very particular attraction, only that she was a little older than him, which was no obstacle at all, but better not kill the tiger not to be afraid of leather.

"Not Alice, for nothing, nothing in particular happens to me, only that I am a little tired of the schedule of the Newspaper. You know that when we do this kind of professional practice, is not much consideration we have, especially when you're just starting the race. "Already the night guards have me tired, I no longer have social life, arrive at the newspaper at 5 pm every day except

Mondays, and then go out at midnight. I'm tired of this," Rodolfo detailed in the commentary to illustrate beautiful Alice well. "

You know what? I heard that I was about to start a Television program, and they are looking for someone young with talent to talk and knowledge of sports", Alice suddenly said, managing to attract Rodolfo's attention, to which he replied: "For the love of God, you are describing me. That's me, where do I have to go or call?", Rodolfo stood up, joking to go immediately, as if wanting to convey to Alice the emotion he felt for that possible opportunity.

Indeed said and done. The following week Rodolfo presented himself in a casting to be the moderator of a new program of varieties, and as he had recently done the Course to obtain the Certificate that allowed him to speak legally in the audiovisual media, he felt that he had a great chance to do the degree and obtain the position.

On the morning of the Casting day, Rodolfo presented himself in a suit, and as always very punctual. He didn't know why he had always been punctual, it was an almost unhealthy matter. Perhaps because he was first a baseball player, and arriving late to a baseball game represented losing the game. Or maybe because he was a soldier, he was obsessed with punctuality.

At that moment they called him to take position in the chair of the Set. The staff began by placing the Lavalliere microphone, the one they called 'balita', used for studio presenters on Television. Then they gave him a kind of script, to read for about five minutes the "Leads" or headers, and then tell him in regression and start the recording. 3...2...1... On the air......

The test hadn't taken more than fifteen minutes, and to be honest, he didn't do well. Been more honest yet, it was horrible. He stumbled to start, then he was misplaced a sheet of the libretto, he was nervous. In short, he said to himself: "After all, I like the work of the newspaper", and left the enclosure where the casting had been carried out, to go to his usual diligences.

Destiny seemed to be creating a plot for Rodolfo to achieve his goals. His perseverance, his preparation, his charisma, his desire to do things well, for him and for his family, conspired for him to achieve the goals. Everything he set out to do, he achieved. He was a dream maker.

As his origin was humble and simple, but as his mother never said poor, always saw the future with eyes of light, in fact in his childhood every night on the roof of his house, spent hours contemplating the stars and thinking about how to improve in life, based on studies and work.

"It's incredible...as you did, you really have an angel. Rodolfo, my friend the casting's Director told me that you were given the position of presenter in the new television program, Congratulations!", Alice was eloquent and gave him a big hug to congratulate him, Rodolfo was still in shock.
"Alice, what are you saying?" was the only phrase that Rodolfo could say, because he didn't know anything. "Oh my God, I did it again," said Alice, thinking that he had already been informed.

Alice as a good journalist had many contacts, and in this case as she recommended Rodolfo to attend the casting, she accidentally found out that he had been selected. At that moment they both realized what was happening, when suddenly the phone rings, and it was the production team of the new program to tell him that he had been fortunately selected.

As a joke but it was true, Rodolfo learned that he was selected in the casting, because no one else went to the casting, and as the program should be on the air soon, the TV Producer played with Rodolfo, and was not wrong to the delight of those responsible.

1992

It's said that experience is the mother of science, and after the chapter lived in the month of February 1992, when he was captured as a hostage, henceforth Rodolfo before leaving to cover his guards as a Journalist, was updated by all possible means, it was not the case that he was again the hostage of another similar adventure.

Being a Journalist, innate, and with the internship at the School of Officers, Rodolfo could properly foresee what was happening. He knew what was going on, but he was terrified to even peep his nose again, as far as that subject was concerned. He still did not fully overcome the assassination attempt to which he had been subjected in his time as a cadet and did not want that period of his life to be dusted off.

At this point Captain Lugo was no longer Captain, now was the Lieutenant Colonel, and obviously imprisoned as he was, Rodolfo was no longer in danger, because there was no plan to unveil. But he didn't want something similar to happen to him again because of his meddling, so he better stay calm.

He only talked about it with Don Roberto, who continued to practice journalism in a more relaxed way, without the intensity of a few years ago, and that's why on weekends there was time to create a family gathering which was always joined by Dennys, Rodolfo's brother and Don Roberto's second son. Apparently the attraction for journalism was a virus in this family, because Denny had also dedicated himself to this activity, but from a graphic point of view. He was a high-end Cameraman, who was being fought by the big TV producers of the time.

LAST MINUTE! NEWS IN DEVELOPMENT: 'A group of soldiers are attacking the headquarters of the Presidential Palace and the headquarters of the television channels Canal 4 and VTelevision Channel 8. The second coup d'état would be consummating in less than 9 months. So far it is reported that both television headquarters, have been taken by the group of insurgents, and from now on there is talk of a large number of dead and dozens injured. It was also known that the Bronco OV-10 Planes that attacked the Presidential Palace were shoot down by F-16 aircraft of the Armed Forces. About 500 Officers and NCOs were arrested for the military insurrection, the rest of the participants are fugitives'.

That morning of November 27, 1992, Rodolfo had been more predictive, and even though the events only took place in the capital of the Republic, if they had taken place in the interior, he would have been able to take shelter, product of the habit of updating himself every morning before leaving his guards in the Canal.

Once again the country showed the seams of the wounds caused by external entities, whose intention was to take over the territory, seasoned with a combination of internal ingredients, such as corruption and the inability of the governments in power to diversify the economic potential of the South American Republic. History would later confirm such thoughts.

On weekends at Denny's or Rodolfo's house it was very frequent to form these gatherings and listen to the three of them talk about different topics, especially sports, which was a common point they had. A practically religious fanaticism around Baseball, a particular passion since all his life.

"Dad, you want a cold beer or a rum?", Rodolfo frequently asked Don Roberto, who was a lover of Rum and 'Cocuy de Penca', a drink typical of arid climates since the plant of Cactus with which it is made is found in those regions. It is also homemade or handmade, so it was a bit difficult to find.

Denny and Rodolfo, preferred more beer to refresh themselves while they waited for food in those family gatherings. This is how the Vegas expressed their family unity and the same was done by each family in their weekend meetings in the South American Republic, as good Latinos, they expressed their affection to friends and family. Until that harmony slowly was deteriorating in the families of that country, disuniting parents and children to siblings, and even couples. This was the first symptom of the rupture of a nation.

1994

"Tell me Father, I was informed in reception that you needed to talk to me, i'm late because I had to mount one of the notes that goes tonight in the breaking news."

The greeting corresponded to Don Roberto who was for some months the person in charge of production of sports news of Channel 20.
"Yes Roberto, I wanted to tell you that I have assigned you the journalistic coverage of the national youth games, knowing that you are in charge of the sports segment in our news," said Father Ocampo.

"But also as the games are developed near the city of Sare, I wanted you to make a visit and one personality Interview to Lieutenant Colonel Lugo Galvez, the coup plotter Commander, who after what happened in February this year is detained in the Penitentiary Center of that city. After this request, suddenly Father Ocampo apologized for having to leave so quickly but had a meeting at the Episcopal Conference. Father Ocampo was an extremely busy personality, so those who have seen, they do like a shooting star.

At this point Don Roberto had accepted with pleasure the assignment, especially for the degree of confidence that the Director had with him, but apparently the most important reason of the Trip to the National Games, was the interview with the Lieutenant Colonel and the subject of the games seems to have been an argument to make everything more natural.

Father Ocampo Iturralde was the architect of everything that the Catholic Church had done in the west of the South American Republic. He was a kind of Midas King, everything he touched or put into it bore fruit. Schools, Media, Churches, Hospitals, even a theme park began to project.

In reality, his ecclesiastical hierarchy was that of Monsignor, only that he and his followers felt more comfortable when they called him Father. He was a simple man, one cannot say a few words, but rather precise words, and who also conducted television programs, and did so in a especially attractive way. He was an outstanding moderator. A man like few gives the story.

After one of the many days of the National Games, one afternoon a commission arrived at the sports concentration, announcing that the bus that would go to the Penitentiary Center of Sare would leave the morning of the following day, and anyone who wanted to visit the Lieutenant Colonel, had to be at eight in the morning without fail at the entrance of the concentration.

Thus, without planning it, Don Roberto was sitting in front of the man who only a few months ago had caused such confusion, in which his son Rodolfo almost lost his life in the middle of that coup adventure. Destiny sometimes makes unexpected moves, and this was one of them.

"Lieutenant Colonel, my name is Roberto Vega and I am a journalist. I imagine that you are informed about my intention to ask you some questions", Don Roberto said cordially, while the leader of the attempted coup d'état repaid his sympathy and replied, "Vega ask me the questions you want, I have plenty of time. The atmosphere had relaxed and with laughter the pleasant conversation began.

Three hours had passed and the gathering did not come to an end, until the organizers of the meeting interrupted and gave them 10 more minutes for the conclusions.

Back at the Sports Village Don Roberto, like anyone who had spoken with Lieutenant Colonel Lugo, did not articulate a word. When they arrived at the concentration, they went to the dining room and then each one retired to rest, since the day had been long and intense. From that moment on Don Roberto would change forever.

1996

"History will do justice. Lugo Gamez is going to win the presidency of the Republic. Our projection is not wrong, besides we have traveled the country by all angles."

The phrase belongs to Don Roberto, who since his visit to the Lieutenant Colonel in Sare that sunny morning in the middle of the national sports games, became an unconditional ally, of that cold and calculating man, whose intentions Rodolfo knew very well, because they were told first hand in the School of Officers.

"The intention of our Commander, name that they began to give the people, is to stabilize the Country. It is to give to each one what corresponds to him", expressed Don Roberto in the middle of the talk, to what Rodolfo said, "You are wrong Dad and the time will give me the reason, by the way the Commander doesn't bother him truth? that guy is weak in relation to the subject of the cult to the personality, and that is a characteristic of the exponents of the anarchy". He ended up almost shouting Rodolfo, in a tone of frustration at seeing how his father, a democratic man, a militant of the Democratic Activity party, was now worshipping a murderer who tried to seize power by force.

On his way to the Presidency, the media literally killed each other to get an interview with the coup plotter, not because his line of thought was very attractive, but because the rating he raised was overwhelming, the product of seeing on screen who caused a disgrace in national life in all his orders.

In that period of time in which the channels exploited the possibility of rating. Journalists asked all kinds of questions to try to bring out the kind of person that was inside that man who had been released from prison in 1994, the product of the Presidential pardon.

Candidate speaks to me please about the government of the Island. What can you tell us of this government, the same one that violates human rights and that has remained in power since 1959." The journalist from the North American media released to the Spanish-speaking public. To this, the nerves of the coup plotter were too evident, but after take a breath, he answered coldly.

"Honestly I consider the government of the Commander of the Island as a Dictatorship, the barbaries he has committed cannot be justified under any circumstances. Everyone governs as they wish, but there are limits and in this case the government crossed the line to become a Dictatorship". Those were the words of someone who just months before had murdered compatriots trying to obtain power by the bad means, in a country, certainly convulsed and crippled by the economic situation, but also besieged by the shadow of the Commander from the island.

"We are here because we will continue fighting for the dignity of the people. With those words, Lieutenant Colonel Lugo Gamez left a marked beginning in his political life even though the phrase had a little defined nuance, because it was not known which people he was referring to, whether the people of the island formed by the clique that took him and held him in power, or the people of the South American nation.

1994

March 26, media literally invading the external spaces of the Sare Prison, a mass of people celebrating that event that brought freedom to the protagonist of the 1992 coup adventures, and 10 of his closest collaborators of that social aggression. Screams of euphoria, joy, and wishes that once inserted into political life, could achieve the goal, in what had failed by arms two years earlier.

The President of the moment, Manuel Calderon, was the one who signed the executive order that dismissed the group of middle-ranking and low-ranking soldiers who had taken up arms against the Republic. It was a decision that was not entirely clear, because in addition to granting full freedom, at no time was he disqualified from exercising political functions. From that moment on, he resumed the MBR-2000 movement, which began as an army captain, and which for years was developing indoctrination and political proselytism in the Próceres Campus, which was the Military Academy of the Republic.

At that moment he felt at the top and invited all sectors of national public life to create a climate of agreement, in fact the representatives of the economic and business leaders, let know their attraction for this person who was going to become a key figure that would mark history, even worldwide. The curious thing was that he never said anything about his intention to transform the State into a Socialist-Communist system. He hide that small detail, he kept his wanderings in the Military School indoctrinating his comrades and for which he was almost expelled from it. That is the reason why the Media wanted to investigate inside the Military, but always knew how to hide the truth as when the American Journalist asked him what he thought about the Government of the Island and the Commander.

On each occasion after talking with his father, Rodolfo sensed that there was something behind it, that everything that was happening was being handled by a 'Big Boss', and his job as a journalist was to get to the bottom of the matter. In order to do so, he had to be in the Capital, because he had the opportunity in front of him, since a television production company in the center of the country had offered him to be a moderator of sports spaces. In this way in the Capital, it would be more feasible that he could get to the bottom, even when he felt a certain fear for what he lived while he was Cadet of the School of Officers. However, the objective would be worth any risk.

"Caramba carajito, I thought that you were never going to arrive, there are suits on the dressing room, check which correspond to the transmission of today and you go to makeup we are to the air in 10 minutes", with deep firm voice and nuanced with the affection of a father, Gerardo Suarez, received Rodolfo with a pat on the back. They were at the headquarters of Deportes Television studios, the company that had hired the young journalist to broadcast the Baseball and Basketball season. "Thank you Gerardo, look there I brought you two pounds of that cheese that you like so much. Put attention because somebody could hide this gifts!," said Rodolfo laughing before going on the air with the transmission..

Meanwhile the Country continued with its rhythm, between normal quotation marks. According to what was seen, with ups and downs, with inflation, with sporadic protests, and with people enjoying their national and international baseball. The political campaign was coming to an end. The two candidates with possibilities addressed the people, one in a tone of advice, on the adventure that would mean electing a coup plotter as President of the Republic, and the other with his discourse of resentment against the productive classes and with a populist discourse, gave an end to their feat and only the decision of the sovereign was missing.

On the night of December 6, 1998, it was known that Lieutenant Colonel Lugo Gamez Riaz had risen with the Presidential Band, the product of 56.20 percent of the votes, in elections that were marked by an enormous abstention, after only 6,988,291 voters out of a total of 11,013,020 registered in the permanent electoral registry went to the polls.

I call on my compatriots not to be afraid. I am not going to install a Cuban-type or communist-type dictatorship in Venezuela. That is far from the truth. The facts will show that all this is a lie. These were the words of Lugo Gamez Riaz after his victory was announced.

Chapter 6

The Republic dies

Rodolfo being in the Capital called Amilcar, his lifelong friend, they had a long time that they did not see each other, that had him a little worried, because the last time they saw each other was before the accident at school, and after that he had to fly out of the country. That's why I didn't know what would be his reaction. "Hello, Amilcar? how are you", Amilcar was guessing who was?. Rodolfo greeted in that way to see what his old friend's reaction was going to be.

Finally, "Oh boy !!, sea bird by land," Amilcar's tone was the same as always and they quickly coordinated to see each other immediately.

"Shut Rodolfo, you are so tough, how you go and stay so long outside, and then come back, and not a single call", the reproach was using a conciliatory tone, but firm, in the sense that he was hurt by that attitude. "Yes brother, forgive me, I know that I did wrong but at that moment everything that had to do with the Capital, left me shocked, that was the reason why I moved away from everything," "But well that's behind and I hope we catch up with everything," said Rodolfo.

That conversation would be just the first of many they would have, and they did not imagine how destiny would turn them into brothers, after living moments of life or death, which would unite them with indestructible bonds.

Amilcar, Rodolfo's childhood friend, as it was typical of the inhabitants of the South American Republic, was very friendly, talkative and charismatic, to the point of achieving what he set out to do. He left a girlfriend in each port, of course in a figurative sense. What was certain was that apart from everything, he was a Don Juan, and taking advantage of this capacity to conquer, he got where he wanted. He had an acceptable appearance, he was not a gallant, or did he have money. He only had the charisma and the verb that emanated from himself and with that he dominated any scenario.

"Amilcar you remember when I was at school I told you about what I was going through, when I did not know how to get out of the problem related to 'Captain'?", said Rodolfo frowning, as trying to evoke every detail of that bitter moment. "Yes, of course I remember", and I remember it so clearly, because that weekend we had two great girls and when I saw you so badly, I left them on board," replied Amilcar.

"Well, brother, I want to tell you that I decided to decipher that package. I want to know what else there is. "On that occasion fear dominated me," said Rodolfo... "It dominated you, no, they almost killed you," answered Amilcar.

"One moment, Amilcar, I never told you that someone wanted to assassinate me. Where do you get that from?" Amilcar went white as a piece of paper, and tried by all means to change the subject, but Rodolfo rose suddenly in a defensive position, only to tell him: "Amilcar that you have done, how is it possible that you are involved in something so delicate and that you have tried to hurt me! and turning around he was leaving the room when suddenly this one stopped him. "Amilcar shouted at Rodolfo, and shook him to make him react.

"Yes brother, we need to talk about many things. You're not the only one who knows pods. This country has become a disaster since that blessed Lieutenant Colonel Lugo Gamez, supported the Trancazo, if since 1989 that guy has been behind everything, but the worst thing is that he's just a pawn. Above him there is a macabre plan that control everything and that is why we must talk.

Amilcar spoke with a lot of propriety, so much so that Rodolfo, at that point was surprised.

"You remember the day you came and told me everything," said Amilcar, "Of course I remember," answered Rodolfo quickly. "Well of the two girls we boarded that night, one of them had gone out several times, with your fulano Lugo Gamez when he was Captain." Amilcar dropped that bomb.

That weekend in 1987, Rodolfo was about to learn everything about the life of Lugo Gamez, who would have been the accelerator of Trancazo in 1989, in addition to creator of both blows in 1992. But destiny made sure that nothing had happened because we don't know what had happened to his life.

Yes, at that time as a cadet he could not decipher what was happening, now as a journalist felt the obligation to move forward, to find the plan that was being developed. Now Lugo Gamez Riaz had won the Presidency of the Republic and was going to develop the communist ideas that he had hidden from the eyes of the people and especially from the media, and that he knew, as well as many military men when Vega studied in the School.

Galvez had made that only visit to the Island to meet with his mentor, had been well camouflaged with a tour of several countries in 1994, whose final destination was that meeting with the Commander. This revealed and predicted the destiny that awaited the South American Nation, if the Lieutenant Colonel managed to establish his project.

"Rodolfo it is necessary that you understand that it's a conspiracy, maybe the biggest one in history", Rodolfo looked at Amilcar with the exorbitant eyes and asked once again, "How do you know that?".

Amilcar took him by the arm, served coffee and started a monologue. that lasted a couple of hours approximately. First he clarified that the day they met, when he was scared to death, he didn't know anything. But then by accident in an outing with the pair of girls, one of which was going out with the then Captain Lugo Gamez Riaz, he had a few more drinks, one of them commented that he was going out with an army captain, and then between drinks would tell the story of who it was. When Amilcar found out it almost stopped his heart, but little by little he began to take composure and continued listening to the story.

The girl was excellent in bed, and it turns out she had the Captain crazy, so one night between drinks he told her some more stories, and the girl absorbed drink like a sponge. She was not very intelligent, because if she had been, she would never have gone out with the Captain again. But some women, especially from the big cities, literally die for a soldier, and if he has troops at his command, apparently that excites them in a way, Amilcar said in a joking tone.

Amilcar continued with his story and Rodolfo listened but without losing a word. "Brother it turns out that after our meeting about three or four weeks later, I go out with Elena", Rodolfo interrupts him, "that Elena...". "Ahh Well, who's going to be a boy, the woman Lugo Galvez was having sex with", replied Amilcar in a mocking tone.

"Look Rodolfo from now on you're going to have to eat wasp, because what comes if we continue in this is not going to be a game. Brother we can leave this right now and nothing has happened, but if we continue we are committed, as you were in the School of Officers. Amilcar was blunt in this. And Rodolfo told him that he was going to continue and that he was going to be more attentive.

"Rodolfo I have a cousin, very close to me and his father is military and works in intelligence. He tells me that they are trying to get Lugo Gamez out of the presidency, because they have discovered that he has a plan with the communist commander of the island. He tells me that they have found communications in which they want to hand over the country's guide to foreigners. Rodolfo interrupts and shouts, "What !!!"

"That's why I tell you that what's behind it is strong, and the country must prepare for what's coming because it won't be easy to get out of this", continued Amilcar .."My cousin has also made me understand many things like, for example, did you know that the island has tried to invade our country a lot of times? Well, the government has always been able to stop those attacks, but now it's different. Before they had done it with their weapons, and the government had stopped them, but now they have an ally in the Presidency and what we can do with that lint," Amilcar was about to finish when he released another little piece to Rodolfo.

"It's said that they are letting the guy run, but at the moment of showing his true intentions, they are going to end that plan and then there could be a social disaster".

And with all of this information, Amilcar updated Rodolfo who was dizzy with all of this. It was a lot of information to pass it so quickly, first had to process it and then think. The situation was dangerous but as a journalist I had to face it. He was finally tying up so many loose ends found since his Cadet days, then when he was held hostage during the Lieutenant Colonel's attempted Coup d'Etat, and now when fate put him back on the path of this conspiracy. 1987, 1992 and now 1998. That man, since the time of Captain of Socialist ideas, passing through two failed coups d'état had become President of the South American Republic. Unbelievable

Ring...ring... "Yes, who is it?" Rodolfo answered his cell phone. "Ummm...ok Gerardo, sounds perfect, let's see how good it's the Heart of Lettuce with Roquefort cheese sauce. See you in a while," Rodolfo said goodbye to his boss.

"Amilcar, the boss invited me to lunch. Let me clear my mind with everything I now know and I'll call you back, but remember zero comments on the phone," he said goodbye to Amilcar then and left for his working lunch.

The new President of the Republic, had become a true autocrat, the power surprised him. Although it is true that they were looking for the Presidency, when the group that commanded it was also surprised, perhaps because of the ease found in the electoral route. This situation would soon make Head of the Country because the people with greater capacity of thought were reading the message, that could not be appreciated in 1998 when he won the Presidency, and it was not that the Golpista could deceive them, the small detail was that on the day of the elections the thinking people decided not to go to the ballot boxes to vote, question that they would regret in the soul.

That February 2, 1999, who received the Presidency of the Republic, was not the Golpista Lugo Gamez, was the Commander of the Island, who triumphantly walked in his first visit to the country, as he had done in 1959, when he came down from the Sierra, on this occasion 'without throwing a shot'.

The months passed and little by little the plans for the delivery of the Republic were unveiled, either from inside the military sector, as well as from the political spheres and the thought called Universities, from where it was possible to measure the consequences of what was happening.

It was then when the different sectors of society became aware of the mistake they had made and trying to amend the cloak, decided to call a national strike, arguing an economic crisis, which was true, but behind there was interest to recover the Republic.

"Hello, Rodolfo?...I need to see you as soon as possible" - said Amilcar.

"When? I can right now!" - answered Rodolfo

"Perfect at four o'clock in the afternoon where we met the last time," said Amilcar again.

He immediately got into the shower and prepared for his meeting knowing that what they would talk about was extremely important, judging by the tone used by his friend.

"Good afternoon, please bring me a cup of coffee. Don't let it be strong, thank you", with a smile sketched by his face Rodolfo asked for something to drink, while waiting for his friend. He took the opportunity to check if he had any messages, but his messaging was completely empty.

"Thank you for the speed of the coffee," said Rodolfo. When he saw how the girl who attended, him blushed. He was a gallant with women. No matter how old they were, he always had an appropriate word to flatter each one. Briefly the girl, about twenty-four years old, stopped to exchange words with Rodolfo, talking about the affluence of people in that place, which was also high. Never that Rodolfo had gone to that place had he found it empty, and it is that it was ideal to meet because it had a special acoustics for the bussines talkers.

At that moment Amilcar arrived, who was accompanied by another person. After greeting and taking advantage of the fact that the girl was there, the new arrivals ordered and sat down, while the beautiful girl quickly went to present the order of her guests.

Rodolfo was the kind of person who didn't expect introductions. He immediately got up and introduced himself to Amilcar's companion. "Hello How are you?, I am Rodolfo Vega to serve you," and stretching his hand tightly to that of the guest. "Hello Rodolfo, Amilcar has been talking to me about you and it is a real pleasure to finally meet you, I am Antonio Herrera, also to serve you," replied the new member of the now group of three.

Antonio Herrera was clearly military, and when you walk straight or limping you are confused. The attitude, the haircut, the way of walking, everything indicated it, and obviously it was the first question Rodolfo asked. At that moment Amilcar interrupted....................

"Let's see... let's see, my brother, let's go calmly. Rodolfo, yes, Herrera is indeed military, but that is not what we want to discuss today. Amilcar was precise and did not hesitate at that moment, for several reasons, among them because he slowed Rodolfo down a bit, and gave his place to Colonel Antonio Herrera, who was temperamental and explosive. That is to say that Amilcar in these first of change had to be a kind of catalyst to to prevent both personalities from crashing

"Lugo I feel happy and pleased to see you now as President of the South American Republic, the one I always wanted for my purposes of expansion, to be able to sustain my ideas and this beautiful project that from now on will grow". That was the phrase, or more than a phrase, was the message that the Commander of the Island Joel Valastro, gave to the recently inaugurated President Lugo Gamez Riaz, as if to remind who had mounted him there in the position in which he was now.

That first meeting was what revealed that the invasion plan was on the right track. Having taken possession of the first magistracy, a great deal of progress had been made. But the subsequent steps would be of much greater care, and for it optimal conditions had to be given, so as not to mistake the move on the chess board. Conquering the Presidency was just the beginning.

Lieutenant Colonel Lugo Gamez had always been an admirer of Commander Joel Valastro. He had read his work, even before he entered the Military Academy, because his older brother was a leftist. Not so his Dad, who magically turned to the left just after his son's first coup d'état. First Mr. Gamez, had been 'Adeco', but as the project of communist invasion did not admit this position, then he decided to change his ideological position as if he were changing a shirt.

The teachers of life that the Gamez Riaz brothers had back in the Barinas of the 1960s, were not others but retired ex-guerrillas, ex-combatants, people who after retiring from the front of struggle dedicated themselves to imparting the word of the left, contravening the norms of an absolutely democratic nation and with attachment to morals and ideas of freedom.

It is in this way how that young man of scarce intellectual capacity, by means of reading and the dreams of figuring in some way, dragging also on his shoulders the economic limitations that he suffered during his childhood, had no other choice but to take refuge in the books of Marx and Engels, induced by his older brother, to adhere to a common plan of subversion, whose purpose was to destabilize. Surprise would be the one that at the end of the road they took, finding that the objectives had finally been achieved.

"Lugo the last time I was in the South American Republic," said Joel Valastro, with a slow voice and something serious, which was his style, "I came to ask for help regarding a quota of oil barrels to oxygenate the Revolution and the response I took was negative. I hope that now I can count on that contribution", complemented the Commander and after a few minutes of laughter, the recently elected President told him, "Just kindly tell me a number Commander, to correspond to such a gesture of solidarity regarding the arms and ammunition that you gave us that February 1989, to begin our path to power".

"I have days without a good night's sleep, I get up every morning, not only because of the habit of my activity, which has always been to get up early and think, when others rest. What happens to me is that it bothers me when I have to know something and I have no way to find out", said Rodolfo as soon as he drew with Amilcar and the Colonel the first of the lines in his meeting.

As always, Rodolfo had come to the point. That impetus was what sometimes blocked his vision, but sometimes caused that he found the goals. At the beginning they had to prosecute many angles and points of view and also points of coincidence. The scheme was so broad, that sometimes there were pauses of silence to order everything. And we are not talking about a plan, because it was already structured, and it was not they who had decided or who were going to implement it. There they were simply coordinating how they were going to control the consequences of what was assembled and what was going to be an attempt to recover the Republic which was being invaded.

It was about executing a general strike, which sought to stop the country, using as an argument the mistaken route taken by the

President, creating new decrees and laws from an Enabling Law that had been granted months earlier by the National Assembly, which sought to place military personnel in all state institutions including PDSA, also sought to expropriate land and businesses, to fill with ammunition his weapon, which was the 'populism', among other arbitrariness ordered from the island.

"Amilcar and Rodolfo, we are in front of an infiltration of invading agents whose only objective is to break the productive apparatus of the country, in order to turn democracy into an easy prey for anything that the group of infiltrators that is associated to the top of the government wants. The fact of placing soldiers in strategic positions obeys the invasion plan that, in complicity with Lugo Galvez, is being developed by the Commander of the Island. In addition to this fact, the President is accelerating the intervention of different institutions of the country, marking more and more the route towards Socialism-Communism intended by his mentor. This brief but forceful intervention of Colonel Antonio Herrera left both of them with exorbitant eyes, especially Rodolfo, because even when he knew where history came from, he was never prepared to compare theory with practice.
"Then what shall we do, Herrera," Rodolfo asked.

To which Herrera responded, "There will be a national strike called by different sectors including the organization that groups companies in all the orders of national life. This body, which gathers the largest number of employees in the country, is alarmed by the recent laws enacted regarding the empowerment of the figure of the President, weakening public powers, in addition to allowing the approval of the new Land Law that takes land from businessmen to deliver them to citizens, I mean the government followers.

These are just some of the 49 laws approved by the President through the enabling law and that are causing this clash between the Government and the productive sector of the country. This is more or less the central idea of the 'project'. It was what Herrera was able to put into words.

At that moment Amilcar was taking the word, "That is not the complete truth, right? that but there is Herrera, you know that I have other sources that have told me that this is the pretext to initiate some actions," said Amilcar clearly and without detours.

"I haven't finished, I'm just beginning to explain, because I don't want confusion or having to repeat," the Colonel said slowly, while taking a sip of coffee, because if there was anyone who drank more coffee than Rodolfo, it was Colonel Herrera.

"God!, the coffee it's over. Rodolfo got up like a rocket, hastening the preparation, because the Colonel without coffee no longer would count the 'project', said Rodolfo jokingly, "In three minutes I prepare a giant thermos but don't stop your speech Herrera".

And Herrera continued. In effect, the plan consisted of concentrating a large number of people at the starting point of a walk that went from Parque del Este to PDSA's headquarters. At a certain point, however, the walk was going to change its route and there the problems could begin.

The day had come. Since April 9, 2002, a general strike and a series of protests had begun to heat up the streets. By Thursday the 11th the protests had turned into riots. As an addition we found a large mass of people who were gradually concentrating in the vicinity of Parque del Este to start a strong march that would go from that meeting point to the headquarters of PDSA. The march had begun and the banners, whistles, Venezuelan flags, waved and sounded to the visual compas of the tricolor flannels allusive to freedom, and the people were already opening their eyes to detect the intervention of the island consequently violating national sovereignty. People continued to arrive at the starting point, leading a march that was aimed at expressing the discontent of the people, at least a large part of the collective, when suddenly !!...

"Amilcar....Amilcar...what's going on," Rodolfo asked after an hour of starting the tour, making efforts to listen in the midst of the loud noise of the people in the heart of the march. Rodolfo had been appointed by the Producer for whom he was providing services to cover the march, but at his own request.

"Rodolfo, I'm not sure... you're listening!..."   - Amilcar shouted.

"Queee!"... - replied Rodolfo.

"I'm not sure, but I think they're taking another route, possibly because there are pickets from the security forces, and they won't let you through to the PDSA headquarters. .... Amilcar shouted again.

While the protest march against the abuses of power by President Lugo Gamez was taking place, around the Government Palace, as was usual when an event was held by the opponents of the government until now, the sympathisers of the same were concentrated. in general they invented any excuse to gather their followers when the sovereign went out to protest.

In the vicinity were the shock groups that had trained the government, which were called collectives and were nothing more than gangs allied with the President who were responsible for dissipating any demonstration. The day passed and the multitude of people that surpassed the million people, little by little was approaching its destiny, but ....which destiny?

"Rodolfo spoke to Amilcar and looked at him with a worried face and he replied, "Brother, this way is for the Government Palace and I don't like this at all.

Then Amilcar ran towards the front of the march and after asking him they answered that there were changes of plans and they were going to the Palace to request the resignation of the President.

Amilcar shouted, "But there are followers of the Government, as we are going to pass," and the answer was 'Not a step back'.

There Amilcar understood that the situation was getting out of control, and that it was better to look for Rodolfo because there would be serious problems. When Colonel Antonio Herrera explained them 'The Project', he spoke of a change of route, but never imagined that this change would be to go to the Government Palace.

Considering the situation and the inequality between the march with more than a million people, and approximately 20,000 elements at the side of the government, among them the gangs supporting the revolution, the fears dissipated a little, especially when Amilcar arrived to where Rodolfo was, and he explained the situation, to which Rodolfo told him:

"Amilcar you are seeing the number of people who are going to ask for the resignation of Lugo Gamez? You are realizing that this is not for anyone; compare we are more than a million people. How many are around Palacio?

However, in spite of the inaccuracy in the calculation of both groups, the difference was that those approximately 20,000 people around Palacio were armed and willing to do anything, while from the other angle there were elderly women, children and of course men, but in their life they had handled a weapon.

In addition, the Government's forces of repression would do whatever was necessary to stop the group of demonstrators, and it was in this way that the Government's protective gangs were distributed along the entire route separating the front of the march and the Palace.

"Herrera, what is happening, you have to update us, because Rodolfo needs to make contact with 'S Television'. The state security forces are attacking the population in a sneaky way. There are people in the march who are falling wounded by firearms," said Amilcar. The Colonel then told directly and sincerely what was happening.

"Guys, this detour was planned because the country is escaping, there are militia groups and agents from the island who are infiltrated, and we must regain control. Herrera, looking around him, continued, "An audio was filtered where the President gave the order to apply the 'Avila Plan', which is about attacking the population with fire in order to control the situation as required, and the Military High Command refused to do so because they considered that this action was against human rights and international laws and respect for the lives of the civilian population.

Herrera ended with these words because he urgently had to get on a helicopter to make a transfer, of which he did not want to speak.

Once the Military High Command, whose command was in charge of Major General Ernesto Marquez Velazquez, refused to obey the order to apply the Avila Plan, the President was automatically relieved, and at that moment he was asked to resign, which he accepted, in order to use literally the same words that the General in Chief and Inspector General of the Armed Forces Luis Rincon, pronounced when, on a nationwide Television message, he communicated that the President had resigned.

Meanwhile , the Vice President for the moment, Captain Diogenes Capelli, was missing, and it was commented with insistence that he had disguised himself as a nurse to be able to escape in those moments of so much turbulence. Later the rumor spread that he was hiding in the Embassy of the Island asking for protection and asylum to that nation.

After the events and the blood spilled, when it was thought that the people had forced the exit of the dominion of the Island, those who had under their responsibility to guide the destiny of the South American Country, mistaken their action, and decided to erase completely the Republic, consequently this error would provoke indignation in some soldiers, who returned to the deposed President, Lugo Galvez, within the next 48 hours, leaving without effect the resignation that he had accepted and signed. This consolidated not only the first phase of the invasion, but also the expansion of communism in the hemisphere, using oil as honey to sweeten those who did not agree.

"At this moment we must remain low profile, because in the midst of the hunt that exists we could be betrayed. That was the central theme of the meeting coordinated by Colonel Antonio Herrera, who was the interlocutor, with the rest of the military who were leading the popular discontent. Those who did not see each other but were the ones who coordinated the discontent of the masses.

"Now that the traitor has been reinstated in the Presidency, they will surely accelerate the merger of both Governments, the Island and the Republic, always under the orders of Joel Valastro," said Herrera, who went on, "Now it will proceed to prosecute those loyal to the population who refused to apply the 'Avila Plan'. We know that the decision of the Maximum Court of Justice, will honor its qualifier, because the Armed Forces protected the integrity of the population, at least as far as the war attacks are concerned, not so much the violence unleashed by the National Guard and police forces that followed to the letter the plan to stop the march that was arriving at the Palace," said the Colonel loudly, updating those present and assessing the moral and material damage left by the event that had failed.

In effect, the Supreme Court released the Military High Command from responsibility, due to the fact that this High Command, by not attending to the order of execution of Plan Avila, did not ignore the government order, but the order issued by the President of the

Republic to assassinate the population with the Application of the well-known Plan. Officers of the Metropolitan Police suffered with different luck, since their commanders were sentenced in some cases for up to 30 years in prison.

"I remind those present that the only objective of our participation has been to restore national sovereignty in relation to the progressive, systematic and silent invasion to which we are being subjected". And after these words Colonel Antonio Herrera said goodbye asking his comrades in arms, and some civilians who had been part of the group, for their strategic usefulness in different operational areas, to rest, that the confrontation was just beginning.

After the events of April 2002, the group that had been in charge of rescuing the country fell asleep in a kind of hibernation, leaving the scene to other soldiers of high and middle ranks, who would pronounce on the matter and accompany the people in the protests that remained active in emblematic places of the capital, and some of the interior of the country.

The Government decided to ignore these emblematic protests, and limited itself to infiltrating tokens and agents to closely monitor any arms uprising. They only apprehended the soldiers who would be supporting the protests, when it was proven that they were calling for the rebellion of the Armed Forces.

Through the events of April 2002, the true intention of the government in office was revealed, which was none other than to hand over national sovereignty to the representatives of the island, a fact that was evident in each visit when they placed the Presidential Band to the top officials of the island.

In all the decisions the brothers of the Island had their hand, from taking the oil for their particular use in energy terms, to obtaining the oil and sell it on their own in international markets as if they had extracted it from their territory.

With the oil at more than 100 dollars a barrel it was convenient to be a friend of the South American Nation, since flattering a little, celebrating the violations of human rights in which his government was involved, or saving the vote in the international summits. some countries could enjoy the benefits of black gold.

The oil issue was a crucial point, because although it was true that the South American Republic was a country with unlimited wealth, it was being squandered in the Island's plans to expand communism throughout the hemisphere.

For the month of November of that year 2002, while the surrender of the country to the Valastro brothers continued, without any kind of complex on the part of the former guerrillas who were now in power, such as for example the new President of PDSA, Eli Ortiguez Manaque among others, the rescue group of the Bolivar's homeland decided to activate after several months withdrawn. This is how Colonel Antonio Herrera once again took the baton this time with a larger and more cohesive group.

"The amount of oil that is being sent to the island without any support is grotesque and has no limits, that is, the oil is being given to Commander Joel Valastro, by executive order, and with the support of the newly appointed President of PDSA Eli Ortiguez Manaque, who is one of the ex-guerrilla fighters prepared on the island, who fought so long from the Sierra", explained The Colonel Herrera, at the time that Amilcar was wondering about this point.

"In this sense the top management of the industry, as expected, is giving a stop to this situation, and this is why both President Lugo Gamez and the Commander of the Island, want to dismember the company by placing military tokens of their environment that obey direct orders, so in this way would be no control," explained with justified concern El Colonel.

At that moment Amilcar, who knew everything that was planned, intervened.

"This event was carried out through a national strike of activities, together with protests and marches in the capital city, forcing the detention of everything until making the President who does nothing but obey orders from the Island, resign. Already the entities of the productive sector of the country are in agreement and they are joining efforts so that this time we achieve the objective. The media is also aware of this, and will support it. In addition, the military high command is on the side of restoring national sovereignty, which is currently suffering an outrage never seen since the time of independence," said Amilcar.

"The project is intended to prevent the continuation of the bleeding of the nation's oil industry, in addition to stopping the underhand invasion of which we are the object.

At that moment Rodolfo intervened, pointing out that according to what he had read, this was not the first time that Venezuela had granted Petroleum to the Island. To which the Colonel replied:

"If Rodolfo is true, the help of the Government of the South American Republic to the Island was true, and it happened for a short period, which began after the overthrow of the Right Dictatorship of Mario Perez Amenez. That energy contribution was made to support Commander Joel Valastro in overthrowing Dictator Basista. But that was a blunder, knowing that whoever takes power by force will never be able to respect any pact. Since then, the Commander has badly forced that aid to be maintained, even trying to invade the country by the coasts of the center of the country. That's why changing his strategy he supported Lugo Galvez from the beginning to obtain the power and now he is collecting that aid. That's the story", I end up sighing for all the exhaustion that this issue generates for the honorable military like him.

"Friends, I am also telling you that this 'nothing' through telephones or technological devices. Hermeticism is necessary. Our group is doing the right thing, Amilcar your discretion around your political group, and you Rodolfo you are the newest to call it in some way but you are very valuable for your military experience of the past and your ability to analyze social facts and let's call it that, your intuition to tie up loose ends", Herrera spoke in a firm tone and when he did he looked directly into the eyes of his men.

"History will reward our action, just as it will reward those who join this cause", and with a handshake the meeting ended in which the role of each of the members who would be trying to recover the Republic was outlined.

Last Minute Breaking News !':.......
'On the last minute news it became known that the oil freighter 'Pilin Leon' was finally stranded in the middle of Lake Marabo in protest against the orders issued by the central government, to give 100 thousand barrels of oil to the government of the island. This situation is extremely outraged to the common Venezuelan and the members of the state oil company.

This is the reason why PDSA's top management has decided to start a strike to stop the flow of oil that is weakening one of the most productive oil companies of today. The Oil stoppage has been absolute, to the point of provoking that the Country is totally stopped'.

Words more or less, that was the matrix of opinion of the media, around the 'Oil Strike' or 'General Strike' in the South American nation, and the headlines of the press identified the protest with both titles, because one led to the other. In addition, such an event after the misnamed April coup d'état was powerfully drawing the world's attention. In fact, the international channels were already being installed in the country to cover the events.

While this was happening, the rest of the country was stopped, due to lack of fuel. However, the climax of the oil strike came when President Galvez challenged the country and dismissed 17,000 oil industry workers who had joined the protest. The president called 'coup plotters' who, with good reason, refused to continue delivering free oil to the Caribbean island.

The argument of the top management of the fifth oil company in the world, was that if the company continued on the road it was going, it would end up bankrupt, due to the interference of the Commander of the Island, and due to the complacency of President Lugo Galvez in relation to continue giving them the oil with the justification of the exchanges of sports coaches or doctors, without any type of studies. This was unacceptable because it was a scam for people.

In the midst of the oil strike crisis, Rodolfo, who was involved in the efforts to recover the sovereignty of the country, interviewed for the media, several experts in the field to explain several points, among which was why once Lugo Galvez in power, the price of oil began to rise. Another question was why in this moment of internal war crisis in the South American Republic, oil collapsed in international markets, if on the contrary everywhere when there is conflict prices rise.

Rodolfo was with one of the most renowned oil experts in the hemisphere. It was Roberto Utelón Berti.
"Rodolfo, if there's anything I can do to help, I'll be here", kindly received the journalist.

"Thanks Engineer. Could you tell me if Lugo Galvez was a coup plotter who rose to power several years after, why the oil began to rise in the international markets, once he took the Presidency?" Rodolfo asked in a straight line.

"The explanation is simple. Lugo Gamez, being the promoter of two coups d'état and then ascending to power, whatever you call it, has meant no guarantee for any government in the world, let alone in the hemisphere. In this sense, if the richest country in the continent is in the hands of a person with that backgroung and communist ideas and in addition this is allied to the Commander of the Island, it is logical and even a mathematical calculation that the oil tends to rise, since at the moment that both leaders decide to lower the production quotas we would be in the presence of the magic oil rule: The higher the production, the lower the prices. The lower the production, the higher the prices", said Engineer Utelon Berti, practically as if it were a table of chemical formulas.

"Engineer another question would be why in the middle of this crisis, oil prices are falling, in fact it's in the low range of 20 dollars per barrel. Normally in crisis the price tends to rise", asked Rodolfo with excellent mastery of the matter.

"In this point the United States has something to do, since in view of the crisis in our nation and the fear of a war in Iraq that could destabilize the markets, the U.S. Government has announced an increase in its crude oil reserves and this has caused the price to remain low. The oil expert concludes.

"One last question Professor, and in your answer I would like you not only to apply your knowledge but also your instinct in relation to the oil strike that continues in the country. This strike is timely, and could be catalogued as one of the ways to get out of the traffic jam," asked the journalist emphatically.

"Rodolfo will speak to you as a Venezuelan, rather than as an expert. This strike is not only necessary. It's obligatory, because the surrender of our resources must end. The way in which the President has given away our patrimony to other countries has no name. In such a way that possibly the objective will not be fulfilled, but one thing I can assure, asking God I am wrong. If the country continues along this path, our oil industry will be destroyed" and with that fateful prediction they shook his hand, and strengthened their souls because the winds were not the best for Bolivar's homeland.

With the passing of days, the government took control of the situation. Once the new State Directors were appointed, the Government felt the reins in its hands. Despite the fact that the people handpicked by the President did not have any experience in the delicate oil industry, within a few days the country restarted activities, albeit partially.

In the same way, the number of people protesting in the streets of the main cities of the country was decreasing, and with this last factor the Government had defeated, at least for the moment the

National Oil strike, and once the invasive project came out stronger.

From that moment on, President Lugo Galvez would have his allies in the key positions of the industry that was the petty cash for his communist project.
What would come now to deepen his power, how would he perpetuate himself and not lose any election? that would be to be seen.

Chapter 7

The fall of the mask

2005

After the 'Oil Strike' and having placed in the top and strategic positions of the industry people of his confidence, even if they knew nothing about the energy area, the President could send all the oil he wanted to his mentor, and this in turn gave him tools, and experience, to perpetuate himself in power. This was the beginning of a phase of restructuring of the Armed Forces and key Ministries to control each thread of the Republic at will.

Gabriel Diaz was a young lawyer, whose presence in the 118th Regional Command was due to the fact that he was nephew of Brigadier General Esteban Diaz. For some years Gabriel had been working impeccably, fulfilling his duties as legal advisor to the detachment. He tried by all means to enforce rectitude within the corps of officials, work inherent to his profession as a graduate in legal sciences at the university level, but the work was too complex and full of vices established in a way rooted in that world full of mafias, which the common people doesn't know.

Attorney Diaz for approximately 30 years had practiced law, showing honor, rectitude, neatness, knowledge and desire to grow as a professional. However, the conditions of the country, speaking in economic terms, as morals did not lend themselves to being able to continue practicing on their own, they forced him to take a military path that he thought differently.

This was basically the reason why Gabriel accepted the offer of his uncle General Esteban, the same offer that had been standing for many years, but for one reason or another, Gabo had always refused.

Now in the middle of that vortex that meant punishing each failure of the soldiers, the risk was permanent.

"Guard....Guard, here please. I need you right now in my office, a complaint has arrived against you", Gabriel called one of the Guards to quote him, to which he replied, "Doctor but I have an exit to commission". Gabo told him to inform his superior that the legal department had called him.

"I will see him in my office in 10 minutes", were the words of Doctor Gabriel, who turned and went to his office at the end of the corridor.

The barracks in which Dr. Gabriel Diaz was assigned, was one of the largest in the East of the Nation, and it was notorious not only for its imposing structure. Besides, Regional Command 118 was special because it was flooded with plenty of posters of President Lugo Galvez, that was the tradition of respect in the Armed Forces. However, what outraged almost all the career officers and troop personnel was to see the flag of a foreign country waving beside to the patriotic tricolor. This fact, which had already been institutionalized, was a real lack of respect that caused stinging in those who saw that image, which had been generalized throughout the country.

"Tell me Doctor why you need me," said Ortega Gonzalez National Guard.
"Pase Ortega, sit down," said Dr. Diaz in a firm voice, "You know what you did yesterday, right?" asked the Doctor.

"Yes Doctor but that was a necessity I have my sick child and I had no choice" declared the Guardia Ortega Gonzalez with a weak voice while lowering his head for shame.

"Look Ortega, I as a representative of the high command of this headquarter should remove the strips and discharge him. But my condition as a human being tells me that I must give him one last chance. The fact of smuggling any kind of merchandise it's typified by law as a crime against the State. Imagine smuggling fuel," he said categorically the lawyer. "Do this again and it doesn't count anymore, at least not from the ranks of this detachment".
The last words of Doctor Gabriel Diaz seemed to be marked in the thought of Guardia Ortega Gonzalez, who, before leaving the office, turned around and said Doctor, "From now on I am going to change and it won't happen anymore", but Doctor Diaz knew that that was false, whoever started smuggling never stopped.

The chapter that Dr. Diaz had just lived, was our daily bread in the barracks. The problem was that the National Guards had been given a lot of freedom since April 2002, when the loyalty of some to the President, had earned him special consideration from the executive. That game of loosening and shrinking the rope, would slip out of the hands of the Government.

While the military robbed and did what they wanted at the lower and middle level, the situation went further at the top. The good relations that President Lugo Galvez had with the guerrilla of the neighboring country had given certain liberties to the middle and high ranks of the Armed Forces. This was initially going to be a mischief, the fact of letting a 'kilito' pass was not seen as a big deal, even though it represented a large amount of money. But little by little, the military opened their taste for the dollars earned in piles and in alliance with narco-trafficking, it would no longer be a 'kilito' with which they turned a blind eye, but would be tons of drug shipments and when the government realized, it was too late to stop what was happening.

At this point a military cartel had already been born, the good thing was that the Southern Command of the United States of America. The media and the U.S. Command itself called it the Suns Poster because it was known that it was composed of several Generals of the Armed Forces of the South American country.

While this happened in the military field, the President was notified about the increase in oil prices, and of 20 dollars he progressively gave a jump until the 60, but in a particularly fast way.

"Adafel, come to the office please, convene a meeting with several of the Ministers, please convene anyone who has a direct bearing on the energy issue. Try not to enlarge the group too much, I want this meeting to be private. President Galvez, after giving the instructions, hung up the receiver and was thoughtful with his sight lost on the horizon, just the look that surfaced when he was up to something, and that was not good news for the country.

Adafel Ramiro, Minister of Energy and President of PDSA, Jorge Armani, Minister of Planning, Nelson Melendez, Minister of Finance, and Ramon Parra Ubaldo, President of Banco BUV, attended the meeting immediately requested by the head of state.

"Gentlemen, how are you? I hope you are well rested because the meeting can be extended", (laughter), we know, we know it well," replied Adafel Ramirez, who was one of the closest to Lugo Galvez.

"You have seen how oil has started to rise, right? well I need to make some measurements and projections because a series of events are approaching and we have half empty coffers. oil has been well below the price it should have. With those words the President made his introduction. "I've heard some stories that I don't like about troop personnel, and I don't want mistakes there," frowning I take a sip of coffee, and get up as if looking for some verbal thread to start the speech I had in mind.

"For the moment the Barrel of Oil is at 60 dollars, but I know that price will soon be surpassed. I've been talking to Commander Valastro and he expects the rise to be slow but steady for the next few months. That is why and following his recommendation, is that I have summoned them today. And exerting pressure on his chin, he continued, "My wish is that from now on, or well from tomorrow, let's start planning. Armani, take note. We are going to calculate the National Budget based on revenues in the order of 60 dollars a Barrel of Oil. In other words, public spending will remain below that amount, obviously we will always have a band of protection to use in the Missions. Lugo Galvez's concentration was intense when it came to numbers, because he knew that was what his populist speeches depended on, he knew that the masses moved with money and with the verb that providence had given him.

"The surplus from 60 dollars, will go to a special area that I will handle at my discretion, of course always with the advice of all of you, but this should not come to light publicly. Let the media draw their conclusions, but I will make public what I am doing, when I think it is convenient. For now that is the main line of action and from there we will execute all the projects we have planned," the President concluded the point and apologized because he was going to the mini kitchen office to serve another cup of coffee, which also was delicious. "He asked, "Do you want a coffee Armani?", to which he replied, "no thanks President I already drank before coming".

Upon his return, the President continued his talk, and said, "We also have some big pending that we must hire soon, and one of them is the population's identification new database, which will be taken care of by Commander Joel from the Island with expert people who will create an identification system for us to know everything. It is a system to create a new database, which gathers the identification, the data of the possession of properties, the payment of taxes. will be known by who votes each person for. We will know everything we need to have absolute control of the population. And that comes with their respective passports, that is to say that it will guarantee us to control any eventuality", with this comment gave way to each one of the assistants, who offered their points of view, obviously not to be taken into account.

The President was clear from the first day that he decided to embark on the adventure of the failed coup d'état and only listened to Commander Joel Valastro, who using it gave him all his support even with weapons and ammunition, much more now that he was savoring the honeys of power.

The history of this plot, has diverse tonalities and although they obey to an only end, it was woven with different types of thread, some stronger than others, but that in equal way they tied and joined to give solidity to the plan.

Consolidated the first phase, whose goal was to place in power the charismatic Lugo Galvez, taking advantage of a population orphaned by a leader, of someone to fill that void of a collectivity that screamed for someone to offer affinity of classes and to convey the feeling of people, to use language 'Populist', now came the strongest step that was to move forward removing the mask, or mask that until now had had the revolutionary process. But in order to do so, but first the process had to have the tools to canalize the river in case it wanted to overflow. And this was based on the principle of 'guaranteeing elections' no matter how. Understanding: Anyway.

"Henry, little brother how are you, it's good to see you. Shit, it's been like 3 years since our last beer", and with a big hug Rodolfo greeted his best friend in the interior of the country.

"Rodolfo after this long time, we are verifying not that we are friends, but that we are brothers, 'pal give me another hug", told Henry from whom we can say that not only is he an extraordinary person, but he is one of those friends for life, and inmediatly gave a hug to his lost brother. By destiny issues he had to leave first to the outside and then to the Capital to develop his career. Rodolfo took the opportunity to apologize for leaving so long without at least calling, but the situation that he lived forced him. But now it was time to take advantage that they were together to share and catch up on so many things.

"Rodolfo tell me how this Bella and Dieguito are? should be adults rigth now !," exclaimed Hector exaggeratedly when he asked for Rodolfo's children.
"In reality, if they are big and beautiful, thank God, and they are from an intelligent that sometimes shock me, in reality all the kids today are like that, but mine broke the mold," answered Rodolfo.
"You could see that they were going to be like that. I still remember Bellita, when she was your key ring, as a child, she didn't leave you in the sun or in the shade," Henry joked with

Rodolfo, and Rodolfo said him, "Bro, I tell you that still it's like that"... hahaha" and they both laughed.

"And how is Mery?" asked Hector.
Mery is the same, physically, but every day I see her more beautiful", answered Rodolfo. and there were laughs of satisfaction from both.

Henry was one of those guys who have a humor that everyone likes and that's why he attracts so many friends, of different level, or social status, but that also has to do with his ability to sell, having been a merchant all his life. He was what we could call a born relationalist. He could have friends who were detectives or policemen, but the same time could have known people who belonged to the mafia, and he still got along well with everyone.

Rodolfo what are you going to do tonight, I want to tell something about Luis Larreal, remember?, I ask Henry, and Rodolfo answered, "Who, the rogue who cheated the University!", respondio Rodofo.
"Exactly, be prepare that what I have for you it's an amazing tale!", answered Henry, and then they met at night to take a ride in his car.

Hunk...hunk...(Clacson sound)

"Hey, coming down," Rodolfo shouted out the window, then kissing Mery goodbye and leaving the house. Once in the car, there was no lack of the habit of looking both sides, due to the insecurity that existed everywhere.

"Jesus !! Henry and this ship, is your or borrowed," said Rodolfo, to which Henry replied, "Ha...ha...ha," and both began to laugh, not without first listening to a picket of tires, as if to excite the day.

Henry did not endure and once began the story that he had. It turned out that this friend of Henry's, Luis Larreal, was a computer Engineer who had cheated a university in the interior of the country, by installing a computer system, which at the end was third category, when they hired him to assemble the latest in technology. With this scam he did he had a few thousand dollars left. and as both knew him, that was the talk for years. Every time there was a scam in the area, they remembered that guy.

It turns out that months ago she had gone to visit Henry and he like a good host, always inviting her friends for a walk. That day Henry called a couple of girl friends, and between drinks they don't know where they ended up, what if I remembered the Gordo, was that Luis had told him that he had created a software to manipulate the voting processes, that is to say to allow altering the results in any election process, and that this had allowed him to have friendship with several characters of the government.

Between the emotion of the drinks and the couple of women who were with them, Luis released all kinds of comments and Henry, who drank little, you could say almost nothing, remembered everything perfectly.

But beyond what happened that night, the next day Larreal appeared in the house to Henry, worried about what he might have said with the drinks, and he replied "Brother what you said is in a grave so quiet, throw leg", after this followed the rumba, so Luis with this attitude, guaranteed Henry that everything was true.

That software was going to be tested in the parliamentary elections in December of that year, 2005, but it was not necessary because the opposition candidates withdrew precisely because they did not trust the electoral judge, that is to say in the CEE, On that occasion, he also passed on the information on which part of the opposition candidates had promoted not participating in a hidden agreement with the government.

At that time there was no way out for the opposition, because if they participated they accepted the rules of the arbitration Institution that was made up of members of the communist doctrine revolution, such was the case of its President until that year 2005 Jose Ortiguez, son of one of the kidnappers of the most famous case in the history of Venezuela. Ortiguez was precisely the one who set up the team that created the new digital platform for electronic elections.

The system was perfected and would be used the following year in the Presidential elections. The firm that they created was called 'Transmatic'. From then on there was no process in wich the result were not adjusted for giving the victory to representants of the goverment.

This adjustments and accommodations of this digital election system it would be what would keep the government solid as a stone, but this situation would turn the government into a declared dictatorship.

"Imagine this Rodolfo," said Henry, "In an inventory the barcode of a product is recorded in a company's system by any application created for that purpose. One product that we will call 'X', for example to a jar of mayonnaise with its barcode, you can change the price in the system. For example, when the product arrives, it costs 4 dollars. Two months before its expiration you introduce in the system that the price must change to 3 dollars and one month before it expires the price in the system will be 2 dollars," explained Henry excited because he had understood perfectly what it was about. That in computer language it's called Programming

"You realize that with the same barcode after programming, you have been able to change the price automatically with the same barcode, right?" Henry explained to Rodolfo, who had already grasped the meaning of the application.

"Well, now imagine that the barcode is your fingerprint, and that the automatic price change instead of being 4$, 3$ or 2$, is an ID number at one hour, another ID number at another hour, and one more time another ID! voilà !", Henry concluded with Rodolfo stunned by the surprise.

"Sure," shouted Rodolfo with his eyes fixed on the horizon, "That's the idiot way they've managed to multiply their votes. And that's the reason why they're never going to lose with this system," said Rodolfo Vega with their eyes first lost, and then see how they were ignited by anger and indignation.

"What a vagabond that Larreal is, what a wretch that guy once faced justice," was the only thing Rodolfo was able to say when faced with the information Henry had given him.

"By the way, Rodolfo, you remember Deisy, the beautiful little butt," Henry said to his friend in an obviously expressive manner.

Of course I'm not going to remember that beautiful back angle," confirmed Rodolfo, who spoke of the same person.

"Well, I'll tell you something delicate. She was dating an American guy. But the complicated thing is that this guy belong to the CIA," Henry commented with a certain complicity and mumbling.

"Henry and what does a CIA agent do in our country," asked Rodolfo strangely.

"The truth I don't know and I don't want to know either. The only thing I can tell you is that she is very sad, because for two months this guy does not appear. He doesn't call, he doesn't write an e-mail, even his WhatsApp is inactive and has never disappeared in that way", Henry explained to a curious Rodolfo who immediately began to make conjectures.

What Rodolfo thought was that Daisy's partner had been discovered and kidnapped, as indeed happened. After investigating with his military intelligence friends, CIA agent Mike Carvajal had been captured by F3 agents on the Island, in a joint covert operation with the elite body of the Dictatorship called the Tactical Intelligence Operations Movement 'Motin', leaving a shopping mall in the capital city. For this reason Daisy had known nothing about her partner for so long.

At the time of the capture he had alleged that he was a religious who was in functions of recruitment of parishioners in the South American Republic. Obviously the Dictatorship was not going to believe that story, so he was immediately imprisoned and tortured. This agent was ultimately going to be key because of the amount of information he handled.

In those Presidential elections of 2006, the custom-made system would have been put into practice, the key that the government needed so much to be able to remove its mask with tranquility. Now they could recognize that the purpose was to transform the system into a socialist-communist one and if any leader, group or political party accused them of being anti-democratic, inmediatly they could pronunce the magic word: 'Elections'! as an argument to stay in power with that hidden fraud.

But doubts remained, there were some inaccuracies, typical of those who set up a process for the first time, and one of these was the certainty that the opposition candidate in the presidential race Miguel Morales had, of having obtained the victory. But curiosusly in the late hours of the night, at dawn he changed his attitude completely. There were those who accused him of having accepted some kind of bribe, but the theory that best adapted to the moment was that of threats to his family group.

However, time would reveal that, between the time of closing the polling stations and the time of giving the results at dawn, the corresponding digital adjustments had been made. In fact in the following days packages began to appear on packages of electoral material burned. The well-known electoral records.

The next step of the plan was to manipulate and rearrange the identification data of the population, with the objective of 'controlling'. In order to do this, they placed in front of all the Registries and Notaries Public of the country, native personnel of the 'Island' with the greatest audacity in the world, because any uprising, they could handle it, with the word 'elections'.
Was the moment to remove the mask and openly declare his intention to convert the Venezuelan State into a Communist.

The country felt a turn in it's core, they were handing over sovereignty to foreign personnel, it was the invasion in its culminating moment. But simultaneously with the oil rising in the markets, they were giving the people free equipment for their homes, developing missions, donations and whatever blackmail went through the minds of the Traitor de Palacio and his henchmen, to keep the population distracted. The opium itself in the noses of the people, while the invasion of the national system of identification was being carried out.

The invaders could obtain the personal data of the citizen, the amount of property, the amount of taxes paid and even know who had voted in any of the elections, because it was an interconnected system that even manufactured the identity card and passport. The serious thing about this for the world, was that from that phase, from the Island they began to grant passports to Cuban, Chinese and even Middle Eastern citizens, who would commit terrorist acts sanctioned at an international level.

Immediately and in order to maintain control over the popular classes, the phase of expropriation of land from its owners began to hand it over to people who most of the time had no idea how to irrigate a plant. This provoked confrontations between the citizens of a single nation as a result of the intervention of an invading foreign country. In this way, with the taking of the date of identification of all the population, the Valastro brothers nailed their Flag in National Territory, and consequently the second phase of the invasion was being completed.

But only one element was missing to make the Amana in the island the capital of the South American country.
It would be the creation of a undetectable system by the satellite networks of the world?   Would that be the Optical Cable?

Chapter 8
The departure

2008

Frontiers outside the world saw astounded everything that happened in the South American Nation, thinking that it was a source of democracy, judging by the number of elections conducted by the government of Lugo Galvez to date, not knowing that behind everything there was a silent invasion that kept the Valastro brothers in power. But not everyone was deceived.

In the Republic of Columbia, there was a courageous President who was never deceived by the invading communists, and since his arrival to power in August 2002 he faced the government of the South American Republic, which protected the FAR guerrillas in it's territory, and this reason was enough for him to treat his homologous Lugo Galvez with an iron fist since his arrival.

This story of intertwined passions takes its peak when Jose Manuel Zancos, Minister of Defense of the neighboring country and in 2008, in the middle of a cleanup by the army of the neighboring country on the border with Ecuador a group of guerrillas was attacked and killed.

The only extraordinary situation was that the group of rebels had crossed the border into Ecuadorian territory, which would initiate an international protest, that could even have led Minister Sancos to face charges in the International Courts

After that event and receiving a vote of confidence from President Jose Uriche, and to a certain extent to protect him since being President any type of accusation raised against him would take longer than normal, Zancos is appointed to succeed him in the Government House of Columbia, due to the fact that Uriche was finishing his second consecutive term.

"Jose Manuel, in view of the trust I have placed in you, and in view of the work you have done from the Government, during the time that the nation has required your services, I have decided to give you my support so that you can run for the candidacy, to try to be the next President of our country. This was the core of the message that Uriche had given to Sancos, who obviously accepted with the greatest pleasure in the world.

Finally Sancos would be the new President. However, the fact of the attack on the guerrillas was pending situation for the former Defense Minister, specially because valuable information was recovered from the guerrilla leader Paul Rey, and this information had reached the hands of the United States, Because by then the United States of America had several military bases in Neo-Granadino territory to fight against crimes in the area.

This fact never was forgiven by the Government of the South American Nation,since a lot of information about the drug crimes was related to the government of Lugo Galvez.

Once Zancos won the Presidency, the first thing he did was to meet with his counterpart from the South American Republic, who up to that moment hwho until then had expressed only rejection and offenses to the former Candidate, now President adding that he was never going to meet with a representative of former-President Uriche.

However, later the autocrat of Venezuela would have to lower his head and go to meet with the new president of the neighboring country. That meeeting was celebrated in Ciudad Tagena, where the meeting was private and secret, and from that moment they were the new best friends.

 Behind the scenes it was learned that in that meeting, both Zancos and Lugo Gamez committed themselves, one to keep certain classified information in some emails recovered from Paul Rey's laptop, and the other to manage with President Radames Correa the issue of the denunciation before the International Criminal Court on the subject of the attack on the guerrillas on foreign soil.

On the other hand Zancos promised to revoke the permits to the US military bases in NeoGranadino territory.

Said and done slowly the North American presence was reduced at the request of the Executive of the Casa de Nariño.

...2011

"Jose Antonio, good afternoon, how are you been, it's a pleasure to see you", Rodolfo greeted Jose Antonio Fernandez, a hard-working man in charge of the administration of one of the most recognized Service Stations in the west of the country. Rodolfo wanted to reveal what was happening, because the production, distribution and sale of gasoline it was literally a disaster.

"Rodolfo right now I'm not even able to talk. Here are the National Guards pending everything and I can not stop, if you want to give me a little time to speed things up and we talked to explain what happens. I can't do in front of these thieves uniformed in green, "So clear were the Antonio's words. Rodolfo told him that if he would wait for him with pleasure, that he would not rush that he would be there to talk with him.

In the meantime Rodolfo took note and with the ability of the journalists with a sense of smell began to talk with one of the guards, telling him that he had also been a soldier, with which the Guard felt identified, a few terms of closed order, mentioning squad and platoon and promotion to which he belonged, and gained his trust, to the point of leaving the service station crossing the sidewalk, to share a cigarette.

"Sargent, or can I call you Oscar?" Rodolfo asked his new friend.
"You can call me Oscar, no problem," replied the Soldier of the National Guard.
"Why this disorder in the sale of fuel, is not understood, we produce and distribute?," asked Rodolfo and the Sargent replied laughing, "The truth is that I am here fulfilling orders, but I know that there is not much fuel, the one that arrives by ships from abroad is diverted and disappears, is the only thing I know".

That was the response of the soldier who was accompanied by a colleague of lower rank, whose job was basically to avoid fights among the population that queued up to buy fuel.

In one of those, the Guard told Rodolfo that he must leave because there was going to be another fight, and he quickly crossed the street to get there on time and avoid a handed fight between two citizens.

At this time Mr. Jose Antonio had finished his work. The time was opportune to invite him to the office to explain why the disaster, and also to tell him that this situation had a lot of time, and it was going to get worse.

"Rodolfo, I'm going to be brief. The situation is that the military is smuggling fuel across the border. It's a more lucrative business than drug trafficking," Mr. Jose Antonio told Rodolfo who frowned as if to say he was teasing him.

"Don't look at me like that, it's the truth. I'll explain, in the simplest way. A tanker full of gasoline contains 38,000 liters. Each liter is marketed to the public in (1)Olivar.

In short, the liter of fuel costs 0.000001 cents of a dollar, using the exchange rate of One million olive groves, explained with all the experience of the world, who for 40 years had held the reins of the oldest fuel business in the city.

"Rodolfo when you multiply 38 thousand liters of gasoline by 0.000001 cents of american dollar, gives you 0.038 cents on the dollar the total cost of the cistern. In other words, the cost of all the fuel contained in the cistern is less than half a dollar. The military are directly diverting the Gandolas of gasoline from the port, to the border where they commercialize it at international prices," Jose Antonio continued his explanation.

"The price of gasoline in Columbia is 0.80 cents of a american dollar, which means that the soldiers selling it for half, 0.40 in the border, they are having a profit per tanker truck of approximately 15 thousand dollars. So I ask as a businessman, what part does the government not understand," Jose Antonio thought aloud, to which himself replied, "The Government understands everything, but the soldiers are the ones who keep that government in power".

Jose Antonio finished his story, and apologized for having to return to the pandemonium he had at the Service Station. He said goodbye with a handshake, and Rodolfo thanked him enormously for the time he gave him.

Rodolfo immediately took stock and thought that this business was more profitable than drug trafficking, as long as there was obviously raw material, i.e. gasoline. But what would happen when there wasn't. Would that industry be stopped, or would that anarchy continue in the border zones between the South American Country and the sister Republic.

His mind was opened to understanding and now he could gauge why the military were never going to straighten out that mistake, at least as long as they could take advantage of that industry. He immediately felt like talking to Gabo, since in his efforts as a lawyer for Regional Command 118 perhaps he could shed more light on this issue of smuggling and he quickly went out to try to find it.

"Hello Gabriel, are you busy," he asked with an emphatic tone, as if telling Gabriel intrinsically to receive it yes or yes. On the other side of the line felt the Doctor, as sometimes in a mocking tone Rodolfo called Gabo, when he said, well I have no more escape, "Come but bring coffee here because it's over, there is no coffee here," perfect I arrive in a minute I'm outside," said Rodolfo, and Gabo replied, Shit".

When he arrived he was most shocked to see the flag of another country raised in the barracks in addition to photos and posters of President Lugo Gamez, "God brother will be possible that one to enter here has to see on so many posters to those people, is not better to place images of our heroes," said Rodolfo in a tone of disgust, and continuing his entrance to the office of Gabriel, I greet him with a hug.

"It's good to see you and know you're okay. Gabo, I don't take up much of your time, I just wanted to talk a little bit about the subject of fuel, and in a whisper-like tone, Gabo replied, "Rodolfo, that's what you came for? Let's go out and talk outside, I'll kill you, what balls you have". And closing the door they went to the nearest cafe.

Already in the car Gabriel asked him if he wanted to get in trouble and recommended that he not do that again.

This issue was exhausting for him becuase every day there were complaints, even the Guards fought among themselves to be assigned in the border area, and what they did was organized to take turns, so that in that way they would get a period for each.

"This situation is getting out of control, because those who lead this type of smuggling are not the Guards or the medium planes, they are the Generals and Colonels who have control of this mafia", that was the answer to the question Rodolfo did when he entered to his office, that is why he practically ran out of the barracks.

"And what do they plan to do," Rodolfo asked.
"I don't know the truth and I'm not very interested in finding out either, because it could be dangerous. If I tell you that the levels of corruption and smuggling are putting themselves on a par with drug trafficking, where there are also military personnel involved. Rodolfo I'm sorry but I don't answer any more, you're gonna make

that they kill me, like they did with 'Pepo and his son'," Gabo said quickly.

"Who they are," Rodolfo asked.

"God Rodolfo, they are not, they were. Pepo' was a former police commander who was killed next to his son after leaving a religious ceremony, as revenge for the gasoline mafias in the border area," he replied with a look of nostalgia because the officer he was talking about was one of the most honest in the police department.

"I have to go back to the office, I have some cases pending," and going to the barracks, Gabo asked Rodolfo to be careful because he was investigating mined land. Everyone was involved in the mafias, both gasoline and narco-trafficking.

The 2006 elections had served as a rehearsal for perpetuate itself in power with an electronic system absolutely manageable by the government. Each election process was going to be adjusted according to the needs of the moment, that is, according to the opinion matrix, the volume of voters in the street and the forcefulness of the work of the opposition.

A system that would be shielded with the point of the plan that was missing. The Optical cable 'that would take to the Island Internet for its inhabitants'. At least that was the argument used not to raise suspicions.

The laying of the cable took about a month in its first stage and then a week, carrying a fragment of the cable to Llamaica, who had the purpose of hide the real intention of the project. Thus, in 2011, the laying of this cable was concluded with the objective of interconnecting both countries, the South American Nation with the Island, in the digital order, and was the culmination of the second phase of the invasion begun in 1998.

In spite of the varied and sought after arguments, all the experts agreed that there was nothing good behind that international project, but very few were able to detect at the moment which was going to be the macabre plan controlled from the Island.

Prior to the installation of the last link of the plan, in 2007, the government requested before the State organs, which were basically under its mandate, the realization of a referendum to consult the population on its proposal to reform the Constitution and deepen its socialist project.

Already with the assembled system, this consultation process would become the bait to avoid any kind of suspicion. That is, any doubt about the accuracy of the system, would be rebutted with the result of that consultative process won by the opposition sector

In the midst of it all, this victory was going to be a kind of gift that the new electronic voting system would make, as if to make it clear that the system was reliable for both sides, because the event that the Revolution really needed was the next referendum where the perpetuity in power of the Valastro.y del Galactico brothers would be approved, as they were beginning to call it.

That is how in 2009 the Government of Lugo Galvez requested a new Referendum where they would have to compulsorily win in order to eliminate the limits to the re-election of public offices established in the Constitution of 1999. The vote took place in February 2009 and the "Yes" won with almost 55 percent of the votes. With which the current President and file of the Communist Revolution, was enabled to run for the Presidency forever and with the armored system of electronic elections, the work was completed.

"Look Gonzalo, look there for a knee brace. I have a nuisance that won't let me walk and we have to solve it because we have to go on tour. I must also meet with Comandante Valastro to begin coordinating next year's election process. I also want to see Vilma because we are going to sign some agreements with the Odetec company, which has behaved with 'Vilmita' in an special way. Galvez had finished asking for his knee brace, joking as he had always been accustomed but in turn showed that the discomfort was still there, despite the anti-inflammatories that had been supplied.

"President, please remain seated, you can not be as always dancing to and fro in the plane as if nothing happened. We are all quite worried and we have to do deeper revisions of that knee". This was what his inseparable comrade Tomas Dabajuro called his attention, who was acting as his chancellor, who scolded the President for the little caution he had at the moment of taking care of his physical integrity.

Many people close to him, wondered why Tomas Dabajuro was so close to the leader of the revolution in the South American country, and perhaps this was due to the orders of the Island since it had been formed with the communist doctrine of which Galvez had only a primary level, through the reading of Marxist texts and verbal brainwashing.

What is certain is that he did not leave alone it neither to sun nor shade, to the point of provoking the estrangement of the closest men and who were with him at front of the military assaults that they protagonized.
What would be the interest of the Island? Were they preparing Tomas Dabajuro for something? Only destiny could reveal what was going to happen.

After the arrival to the great nation of the south where the 'Samba' reigns, President Galvez felt a little more rested which gladdened the group that was on tour. The President had his coffee removed from his diet, and instead every time he ordered coffee, he was given a rosemary tea or a linden tea.

Thus things began meetings with the Latin American giant whose relationship with the different governments of the continent was exaggerated. In the past no company had had so many relationships with so many governments in the Americas, and later you would know why.

"Dilma of my life, always beauty like a spring flower that blooms in every exit of the suuunnn", was the improvised stanza that President Galvez had sung to his homologa Vilma Yusef, who was also fluttering as if stunned.

"Hello Lugo thank you for being with us, come sit down and stop those things that blush me," she said with a blushing face, and not precisely because of the makeup. "I hope the trip was relaxed," she wished him and he replied absolutely yes, it was excellent.

"Look Lugo I introduce you the representative of the company that has better relation with our social ideals, the Engineer Robertinho Tunja". Vilma made the respective presentations and immediately began to draw up strategies, but above all to number and coordinate dates of contracts, starts of works and advances of money to be able to execute.

The company in question was a monster that had expanded actions throughout the continent. With offices in the North, this construction group won bids right and left, literally. From the stadiums of the World Cup Brazil 2014, to the remodeling of works for the 2016 Olympics that were also going to be developed in the colossus of South America.

This company could build everything from sports palaces to social apartments to satisfy its clients. Due to this versatility they were considered the giants of the American area and therefore an ally of the governments of the moment.

Then began the phase of offering payments, with dates, and the very important commissions, remembering that always the chancellor Tomas Dabajuro was present briefcase in hand to assist every decision and every action of its President. Thus began the dance of millions, corresponding to payments for the concept of hiring different works to be performed in the territory of the South American Nation. Even though it was a preliminary meeting, everything indicated that they were going to be taken to the thousand wonders, since they were equal interests, like 'cutted by the same scissors'.

To all of these, the oil continued its escalation and at that rate the laughter of the Latin American hierarchs increased. The effect was like a rule of three, the greater the rise in the price of crude the contributions of the richest nation in the world in terms of black gold were greater for their allies in the area, and that meant virtually free oil for anyone who had scored in the expansion of the communist project of the Valastro brothers.

When everything was in order, more meetings were planned with the construction company, which would take place in the courtyard of Lugo Galvez. "There I wait for them so that we can eat a good piece of meat on a stick or a grilled pork, well if Dabajuro leaves me", in the middle of the laughter those were the words that the President offered to his new friends while was boarding the plane to continue his tour.

As soon as the Presidential plane touched down, it was quickly received by an unusual commission in these cases. Usually you find the chancellors or the President. This time the South American president was received by a team of paramedics, before the previous announcement of the President's malaise. They quickly transferred him to a complete revision type 'A' since the problem of the knee persisted and they did not want to neglect anything. The plans were going perfectly and they did not want an unforeseen event to ruin the progress the Island had made around the seizure of the South American country.

Once there, they asked the group of the third and second safety ring to withdraw for the comfort of the patient, but the first ring remained immovable, including Tomas Dabajuro, who remained at the side of his partner without separating.

After four hours of intense studies, the source of the president's problems was known. It was a moment of great tension but nobody imagined the diagnosis. When the doctor gave the result of the studies all were petrified, as if they had announced the launch of a nuclear bomb.

"Gentlemen, after having made the complete examinations to President Galvez unfortunately the news are not good", said Doctor Remigio Cundriolo, Internist, but also specialist in Oncology. "He has a tumor in the lower part of the thoracic cavity, and this tumor has malignant cells, according to the studies we have done.

Suddenly began the nervousness, the lucubrations, the conjectures and the possible predictions, that naturally are made after this type of announcements.

"Wait a minute, we can't do evaluations a priori. The tests must be performed again in order to be certain", intervened Paul Valastro, who had been notified and was in a special room in the hospital where the patient was located Galvez.

"Before performing any other exploration, we must wait a certain period of time, for reasons of medical protocol," said Dr. Remigio and rose leaving the room.

The atmosphere was one of complete surprise and anguish: "We must inform the country about what we are doing," said one of the members of the delegation.

"NO.....absolutely not. We cannot show signs of weakness before the country, much less when we are abroad. We must wait hermetically", said Dabajuro and immediately they began to census the attendees, and check their respective telephone sets. They found it necessary to carry out all those controls to prevent the filtration of any photography or of any information relative to the super powerful Lugo Galvez Riaz sickness.

Meanwhile in Venezuela a tense calm was maintained. During the President's trip, a segment of the population, the one that opposed him, limited itself to protest by means of criticisms to the management and to the interferences of the brothers of the Island.

Conversations in the public transportation, in social network post, in the queues of the banks, in the markets. The people were aware that they had erred in many things from the beginning. Since that fateful 1998 when by punishment the old politicians stopped going to the polls, and even in many cases gave their vote to the Golpista who put in check the tranquility of a nation.

Several days passed and the examinations were carried out again, taking more time in their execution. They even performed extra tests and some procedures with more advanced techniques, but the results were exactly the same. The second diagnosis revealed that Lugo Galvez had a tumor with malignant cells. In common terms, he had a cancerous tumor.

To all the people around the first mandatary, the problem was. First how to tell the President about his condition, and then how to make the announcement to the country so as not to lose control of everything. A large part of the population was going to take advantage of the situation to start a new phase of mobilizations and that terrified the members of the government...

The first step was to tell the President, but any effort to draw the information was in vain because he was fully aware of what was happening, in fact when they tried to tell him what was happening, he told them quietly: "I already know everything, but the team wins".

"But Commander, how did you know Sir.," asked Dabajuro as he locked the door to the luxurious room. "Simple common sense, and with the help of some compliments to the nurses," replied the President.

"Now Dabajuro the most important thing is to think how to inform the population without creating panic", Galvez thought out loud and that is that the President in his delirium of grandeur swore that the people continued to love him as on the first day, as that afternoon when he left the Sare Prison, or as when they lifted him on their shoulders to take him to the Government Palace. He did not realize that the dominion exercised by the pair of the Island had caused his beloved people no longer feel the same for him. That surrender of the homeland to another nation, the two flags waving in the barracks, the institutions of the state in the hands of agents of the Island, even agents infiltrated in the barracks of the homeland. All these factors, in addition to giving away the patrimony of the Venezuelans, had caused his popularity to drop to levels never seen before since he launched his coup adventure.

Now facing death he could see clearly that he had failed his people. Same people whose yoke the great Simon Bolivar eliminated, and that now he had allowed to be installed again.

There were so many reflections in such a short period of time. And Galvez thought loud, "Perhaps there can be an opportunity to redeem myself with my people," but that thought heard by a third party, provoked the most vile act of treachery. Dabajuro, speechless, heard what the President said while his gaze remained fixed on the sky.

It was too late. That one person who had understood the emotions of those who, facing death, wanted to reverse their baseness, would speak, sing like a canary announcing that the leader should disappear.

"President, what are you saying? Do you intend to throw it all away?" Literally expressed Tomas Dabajuro with wide eyes and a pale face like a bird of misfortune. "I do not want to think that you are sorry for everything we have done to consolidate the conversion of the Republic into a socialist state." Dabajuro was facing nothing more and nothing less than the President, to which he responded: "It's not about that, it's about balance, an element that has been absent from my decisions, it's about doing things with a little more than nationalist sense ". Galvez finished the sentence and sat in bed because the treatment he had started had weakened him.

It was known that the problem of Lugo Galvez Riaz was complicated by the region where the tumor was housed. But it was also true that with the necessary care and attention in more advanced health systems such as the European or North

American, the President could come out of his health situation better.

However, the political position he had maintained towards the 'Empire' countries did not allow him to go in search of help to any of them that had the resources to save his life. On the contrary, he decided to stay in the hands of those who had managed his life since the first day when he made the decision to participate in the project to take over the South American country for its transformation to communism.

The methodology used by the Revolutionary Government of President Lugo Galvez Riaz, had been based throughout its existence, in the millimetric planning. In this sense, the arguments that were going to be used to make the information known to the people, had to be dosed and guided by the experience of the Island Regime.

In order to give explanations about the state of health of the National President, they used his fabulous apparatus of mediatic manipulation. But that first bulletin had to be the most important, the one that left no doubt that what happened to the President was something fleeting, and for that they had to unload the attention of the 'populo', for which reason by that time they had the brilliant idea of freeing Two thousand inmates from the jails of the country, with the argument of the reinsertion to the life and the production of the Nation. That was fantastic in two ways. The first was for the use that could be given in the future to those gangs or groups of delinquents that were freeing, obviously under special conditions of loyalty to the Government, and the second was for the powder that would be raised, with which the importance was reduced, at least in the popular classes, to the first bulletin where it was said that the President had been intervened, obviously without mentioning cancer.

From then on, it would be a libretto in relation to divulging with delay everything that happened with the President, that is to say that they divulged the first fact, when the second had already occurred. They were diluting the second event when the third had already occurred, and so on, in order to have space to maneuver in the event of any eventuality, as indeed it did.

The country followed its routine, between daily problems and protests, between insecurity and the population's desire for tranquillity. But there was a crucial factor for the communist project that was being conceived and that was that Lugo Nataniel Galvez Riaz, had to face presidential elections within 16 months. The most important elections around the transformation and seizure of the South American Republic by the Small Communist Island.

How could the government of the island and the revolutionary government of South America heal the charismatic leader who had given them everything on a plate? They had to structure a master plan to make the adjustments with millimeter precision. What would that plan be?

...2012

"Yes Dad get relax, I'm not going to get into trouble, don't worry, see you soon", Rodolfo reassured Don Roberto because he had been in the Capital for a few weeks covering a vacation, and Don Roberto was a little nervous lately, due to Rodolfo's political involvement.

That year 2012 was being quite complicated. On the one hand, the population knew that the President was still in bad shape despite his pretense of wanting to cover the sun with a finger. The use of steroids was evident, side effects that caused him tremendous facial and body swelling. However, with the risk of dying in the attempt, he was going to run for re-election. Only that the elections of that year were going to be different.

Due to the illness of Lugo Galvez, the CEE had advanced the same ones to please the request of the Island and of the own President. Perhaps it did not would reach December, so it was imperative to make them in the month of October.

While this painted the political landscape, certain issues that had remained classified during the twelve-year term of government were being dusted off. There were suspicions about certain irregularities in some topics, but it was not until Interleaks unveiled a thousand state secrets that many theories were confirmed.

The subject of Uranium it was neuralgic at world level, due to the fact that a specific country such as Chizan was, at that time it was working to develop nuclear plants. Chizan was in the sights of the

States Together, due to its nuclear attempts. In addition there was proven request for help to the scientists Kursos for the manufacture of plants.

It was then that it was proved that the South American nation had been selling enriched uranium to Chizan for the purpose of creating nuclear weapons. The suspicions had been based on Chizan's interest in establishing cooperation agreements with the government of Lugo Galvez. Through the creation of a tractor factory that never began operations and through which a large amount of dollars entered the country. Also a 'Fake' was used around the extraction of the Gold, although it was true, it was not the only mineral that was extracted.

This was easily verifiable, by the refusal of the Government of the South American nation to allow over flights in the area, in addition to the construction of an airstrip of more than two kilometers of extension for the takeoff and landing of planes of great importance, used for the transportation of heavy material.

When the government of the Republic Carioca returns to democratic hands, that is to say when Vilma Yusef, is deposed as President product of an 'Impeachment', the sheds used for the supposed factory of tractors were immediately dismantled and also the track was destroyed and all the evidence of the activity of extraction of the presumed Uranium, simply because the new government, being contrary to the interests of the San Bailo Forum, was going to allow overflights at the border level, which would reveal the activity developed around the material for nuclear use.

"Amilcar, each step taken by this international band has been coldly calculated, with no margin for error. In each subject there is a team of experts that has been prepared for this purpose, and apart from this investigation that I am carrying out, there is another related to international terrorist groups of Middle East". These statements made Amilcar tremble, listening to every word that Rodolfo spoke.

"Please order the food quickly, I am starving" Rodolfo said, adding, "Amilcar remember don't talk about it at the restaurant. These places are full of people linked to the government, even though they are socialists, they like fine places," Rodolfo said sarcastically.

The President's illness advanced as established in the medical protocols. The type of carcinogenic tumor suffered by the President was among the worst. He was lodged in his entrails, as if providence were on the side of the people of the South American nation, to avoid transformation towards a system that, in every part of the world in which it had been put into practice, even in terms of history, had failed absolutely.

On one occasion, President Lugo Galvez, in the middle of a historical speech, dared to curse the people of Israel precisely from his bowels, for opposing political and military positions, a moment that was now brought to mind after his illness had been diagnosed. On that occasion it was too much anger, rage, bad desires, and offenses that the President pronounced to the Israeli People and those who believe in a superior being obviously qualify the ailments of the leader of the Revolution as a kind of punishment for an event as great as the words uttered in that speech.

"Eli, what will you doing this week? too busy to come with me?" the President asked his Minister of Electricity.

"Not at all, President, of course I'm marching by your side. Allow me to leave everything ready in office", answered Ortiguez Manaque in the most supportive way to the request of his Commander.

Ortiguez Manaque, had been one of the precursors of the communist transformations in the South American Republic. Formed on the island, under the orders of Commander Joel, he was always willing to be at the front with weapons, hidden in the Sierra de Sudamerica, until they silently obtained power. Now he was again at the front marching beside the leader who needed his trustworthy pieces for their tranquility.

"Thank you Ortiguez for your willingness to always serve the cause. From this moment I trust you and my lieutenant Tomas Dabajuro, who will accompany me to this feat to recover one of my most valuable trophies, my health", with those moving words ended his conversation inside the vehicle that had taken them to the airport, where he was awaited by a commission of his Government, to wish him luck in this third surgical intervention to which he would undergo.

During those turbulent days, the President had the sensitivity to the surface of his skin that had inspired him so much in his moments of oratory climax and with which he arrived so deep inside the people. However, in those moments that sensitivity was tinged with one of the most natural feelings of the human being, fear.

Fear for leaving, for going to the unknown, and above all fear for not knowing if everything he had done guided by his brother Joel, had been the right thing to do. They were private intimate thoughts that he did not dare to tell. However, his attitude and a bad comment made in front of Tomas Dabajuro, had betrayed him and possibly was his sentence.

It was time for the embarkation and he left for the Island. Once again...

"Rodolfo finally established communication with his friend Chala.

"Rodolfo that good to know about you, as these, in which I can serve you", the answer denoted the same tone of confidence and affection.

"Chalita I need a ticket for tomorrow for Miami, but will be just for a week, I have to do a super important interview and I get very expensive direct by the airport," said Rodolfo in an altered and anxious tone.

"Don't worry, Rodolfo, I'll have it ready for you in the afternoon and I'll send it to you via e-mail, I will tell you that it's going to come out at almost half the price in relation to the Airport...kisses", said Chala.

"Thank you Chala, I knew I could count on you, talk to you later...by the way you sound younger...hahaha... don't panic I am kidding", and in the middle of the laughter they closed the communication.

Passengers your attention please, the following is the first announcement of flight number 11044 bound for the city of Miami, please board through gate B, international departure hall number 3.

Already in the corridor and about to take the flight, Rodolfo toward the last contact with Dr. Juan Rafael Martinez, who so far had been key to disclose and inform the population the real sickness of the president.

"Doctor thank you for your time, it is a pleasure to greet you, while congratulating you for your impeccable way of informing people about the suffering of the President, given that the government cabinet is unable to tell the truth", at that time Rodolfo in addition to his words, extended his hand to shake that of the Doctor.

"Rodolfo would you like a coffee, perhaps water," asked the Doctor, who was accompanied by his assistant.
"Yes a coffee would be opportune, Thank you", and in this way began the conversation between the two professionals.

Dr. Martinez was a recognized physician who practiced in the City of Miami, and who through the networks had become the lifeline for the population of the South American country. His timely messages in the networks were awaited by millions of people, who saw him as the eyes of truth in the face of so much darkness offered by the government regime.

When Rodolfo precise it and asked about its source, the doctor reacted sourly, saying that he could not reveal who were his informants, for personal and professional ethics, since first of all he was a man of honor and second was a doctor respectful of those who provided information.

The second thing Rodolfo asked was exactly what Lugo Galvez was suffering from, to which Dr. Martinez responded directly.

"President Galvez has three problems. One in the adrenal glands, another in the liver and a third in the bladder area. In all three cases the problem has caused metastasis and is irreversible.

As simple as that. Dr. Martinez explained what the current clinical picture was, and it continued. "In fact, the person who is offering me all the information called me and told me that another tumor of little more than one centimeter had appeared, which was the reason for this third operation. However, when the laparoscopic doctors realized what was there, they preferred to clean the area and not remove it, to avoid complications", with the lost view directed towards a sheet of paper on his desk, Dr. Martinez ended his comment.

According to what Doctor Martinez had told Rodolfo, and according to what the doctors attending the President knew, there was nothing more to be done. The purpose was to keep alive the only man who could maintain the revolution, sadly the one who after his face to face with death, had reflected, but who would not be allowed to turn back and in a master play, the mafia of the Island, had stopped the reverse, just with the time necessary to win the reelection, and execute the 'Twist of the chess towers'.

Page 188

"Doctor, I can't thank you enough for your kindness. Thank you for sharing your time with me," Rodolfo said at the time of the farewell.

"You're welcome Rodolfo thanks to you for the visit, and remember never to speculate about who gave me the information. By the way I wanted to ask you to be objective because lately I have felt that I am being watched and I would not want a lightness on your part," and ending the Doctor with eyes certainly full of fear, said goodbye.

On the way back Rodolfo did not stop thinking about the last words of Doctor Martinez. He tried to review each fragment of the interview, and in fact from a certain moment his tone of voice changed, as if he had remembered some episode, or perhaps some threat. But at the same time he thought that would not happen in North America, a death threat in that country was unlikely, so he discarded his crazy hypotheses and closing his eyes he set out to rest at the Uber that would take him to the hotel, for preparing the interview as soon as possible. He wanted to take advantage of the rest of the trip to visit Dilson, his brother

Benny and some friends and then do some shopping until the day of his flight to the South American Republic.

Given the illness suffered by the President and foreseeing any of the possible scenarios, including death, from mid-2011, he opted to request the repatriation of all the Gold of the nation that was stored in vaults of North America and Europe. The recommendation had been made by the King of manipulation Joel Valastro and his brother Paul, arguing that for any lack of his person, the power could be lost, but before they had to put to good shelter the more than 365 tons of Gold.

And so began the process for the transfer of monetary Gold to the Capital of the South American Republic, while Gold was being withdrawn from the United States and Europe, to be stored in Pina, Kursia and the Carioca Republic. The Repatriation of Gold from the South American Republic, would be carried out with a delay of approximately 3 months from the date of application, and this was due to several reasons including the aspect of security. Also taking into account that the country was with its empty coffers product of looting to which the nation had been subjected by other countries of the hemisphere, it was first necessary to verify that everything was in order and without any claim.

On the other hand, North America was already beginning to scrutinize the embezzlement that some of their public officials were carrying out and within the protocols it had to be certified that after the repatriation of the Gold, there was no claim. Thus, by the last day of January 2012, the entire transfer of the Gold had been carried out.

That move was due to two factors. The first was to try to distract the attention of the people a little on the illness of the President just weeks before the holding of the 2012 elections that were going to guarantee the revolution for the future. The second factor was to try to repatriate the gold and from there take everything to the Island, since if Galvez died the gold would remain in the Island, that is to say that all the planning was to carry out a vulgar looting, just as it had been happening since the beginning of the so-called revolution of the 21st century.

So once the Gold arrived at the vaults of the Central Bank (BCS) brought from Europe and the North America, immediately the plan was elaborated whose execution would put the ingots in their final destiny. It was thus as in caravans of armored trucks via the Airport, all the gold reserves were moved to the Island where they rest in the coffers of its Central Bank.

The elections were barely eight months away and while President Galáctico was touring the country, with the limitations of his own ailments, his opponent, selected after a primary process carried out by the national opposition, came out to the bullring asking for the union of all sectors of society, to shake once and for all the regime that had given everything to the Island.

But as everything was millimetrically calculated, the chances of the government's defeat were minimal.

"Now, George, let's take another look at the agenda. 1.- Directors of Transmatic, 2.- Witnesses of Tables, 3.- Custodians of voting records, 4.- Personnel in charge of the digital equipments, 5.- Optical cable working", said the President. When reviewing the list suddenly the Galvez looked up at the wall clock that he had in front of his desk in the office and said, "In my life I thought to give so much importance to time, every minute, and with a nostalgic look, returned to the page where he is reviewing every detail for the approaching contest, a kind of crusade in which he did not know where the enemy was, or did not know if the enemy was everywhere.

When Lugo Galvez was referring to the Optical Cable, he meant the means by which the CEE Count Room would send the results in real time to the Situational Room in the Amana city, in the Island. In this way they would make the usual adjustments but this time should be in lightning time. That's mean, saving time in delivery to the island and not using all night long how has been happening since 2006 when the President won the elections against Miguel Morales, in a process in which suspicions were raised about the fraud they made with the electronic machines, because of the delay in giving the final results.

The Presidential campaign was relentless and exhausting for both candidates, especially for President Lugo Galvez who aspired to re-election with an unstoppable and inspiring spirit, but a body that was paying the price of abuse for having violated the treatments to which he had been subjected. The culprit was Commander Joel Valastro, who without compassion stimulated his pupil, no matter if he died after the victory.

On the day of the closing, the sky of the Capital City was completely black even though the closing was in the evening hours. It seemed more like the scene of a nefarious outcome, when suddenly and just at the close of his epic began a torrential downpour broke off that took Lugo Galvez by surprise, who could not avoid receiving that impact on his body, which would bill him the following weeks.

At the end of the day his words flooded the concentration, "In our hands is not going to lose the life of the homeland. I am completely sure, and especially that in the hands of the youth is not going to lose the future of the homeland, for my part, I will continue with you because my next government begins on October 8.

Thus, the voting day was intense, only that the strategies of the government group, headed by psychiatrist George Ortiguez, changed in complot with the principal rector of the CEE Yurislay Orejuela. The instructions for the followers of the government, were to execute the act of voting late, to congest that hour of the day. In that sense they could have a chance to alter the results in their favor if the people decided to vote for the opposition candidate.

Yurislay Orejuela, had been precisely the one who had replaced the psychiatrist George Ortiguez, and this relationship was extremely close, which made more reliable any plan established to achieve the objective, which was to keep the dying President in power. Orejuela was always a key piece of the Commander of the Island Joel Valastro, who was indoctrinated and trained in military matters on the island for several decades.

The same condition was presented by the assistant or aide to Lugo Galvez, Tomas Dabajuro, who was indoctrinated on the island decades ago, and who was a dormant cell in the Bolivarian Republic until the invasion plans entered their second phase. Dabajuro would ultimately be the strong card of communism that was sown in the American continent.

Thus the preset plan continued, even late at night, when the multiplication of votes by the government became easier. There were followers of the Revolution of the 21st century, in the voting tables, more or less until 11 at night. At this point the information traveled in real time to the Situation Room in the Island, from where they executed the adjustments by region and they returned them to the counting room of the CEE, to have everything to hand and to announce the new victory of the current President, in the smaller possible time after the closing of the tables. The people suspected and even intuited that the majority had voted for a change, a consequence of the fatigue of the population due to the excesses that had begun to come to light.

The culminating point of the election process was when CEE President Yurislay Orejuela announced the victory and re-election of the President Lugo Galvez Riaz, with which in this occasion the deception was double, due to the lie about the illness of the President, and also in relation to the false results of the electoral contest. The population continued in the lethargy of an endless nightmare.

This scene would serve as a preliminary step for the Caribbean clan to wield the sword with which it would strike the final blow on the neck of the one who had repented of having mistreated his people.

But how long would Lugo Galvez Riaz last in power ?

Chapter 9
Beyond communism

"Rodolfo, tell me how the situation is on the inside, cause the capital continues to be lit, the people do not accept the trap", Amilcar said by phone, who also added that the government was willing to do anything to avoid losing power.

"In effect Amilcar here in the Province is the same, but what the opposition candidate did in the sense of sending people home, was a disappointment. People feel betrayed and confused.. Here it is rumored that once again the President was about to give the order for the application of the Avila Plan, just as he did in 2002," Rodolfo replied to Amilcar.

"Amilcar this rumor its true? Could you tell me you're in the capital," Rodolfo asked.

"It's an unconfirmed rumor, but knowing the element and the people that is around, it's very likely that it's true and I'm sure he wouldn't have shaken his pulse. Total had already done it in 2002", ended his sentence Amilcar from the Capital.

"Already in the Province, there are dead people in front of the headquarters of the electoral authorities. The government have placed snipers who are blowing people's skulls, and the worse is the majority are young university students who know the game with the voting machines and it is not going to be easy to force them to go to their houses", completed the conversation Rodolfo with a contained rage, at the time that was throwing a glass against the wall of his apartment.

The situation was complicated, since the people knew about the fraud, but there were no other international organizations than the cliques of the regime, who being representatives of Asosur, were going to testify in favor of the government. If the people remained in the street, there would be another massacre like the ones that are already habitual on the part of the shock gangs or collectives and the government would wash its hands of the fact, alleging that they would have had nothing to do with it.

Slowly the tension went down due to the physical fatigue of the population, exhaustion that was induced, by means of the cut of electrical energy to the different regions in rebellion, in addition to the control of the gasoline whose shortage they handled to their whim. The regime according to the instructions of the island had everything perfectly calculated. They even worked on the basis of calculations regarding the margins of error, which allowed them to be prepared for any scenario.

"But Rodolfo how could it be possible that the government could adjust the results so quickly if in each voting center there were groups of witnesses super trained to detect any type of trap," Amilcar asked in a desperate tone for the tension that was being experienced.

"Amilcar, they do it using the transatlantic optical cable, which they have installed for that purpose. Those criminals have invested a large amount of millions of dollars to connect the Capital of the Republic with the Island's Capital, using Jamaica as a bridge to disguise the play, this cable is the secret way through which the information of the data of all is crossed, in this case of the results of the elections The data arrives at the counting room and is simultaneously sent to the situation room of the Amana, to make the adjustments, and later return the final information to be offered as final results ".

"By means of this modality the sending and return of data was guaranteed, without any type of interruption and at a great speed", Rodolfo answered with precision each one of the questions of his companion.

"The adjustments could not be made in our city for obvious reasons. Many witnesses, one of the Rectors of the electoral body is in favor of the people, and to do so using satellite communication, was to run the risk that any interference, unveil the plans or interrupt the adjustment of the final numbers," said Rodolfo, who was astonished by what a group that a little more than three decades ago had wanted to invade the coasts of the South American country.

In July 2012, the President had referred for the last time to his illness, guaranteeing that he was totally free of cancer, that he was totally recovered, and it was not possible to foresee another attitude, when in a few weeks he would begin the campaign for his re-election. His island teachers had been precise in their instructions, and the main one was, feel healthy, reflect health and win, because no one would vote for a dying man.

However, after his victory, especially after that epic closing, in which he received a torrential downpour, the defenses of the reelected President, had dropped, and as he was still compromised with his serious health problems, he decided on November 27, a date that was too symbolic for the followers of the 21st century Revolution, to request permission to the National Assembly, of official majority, to go to the Island in trip of more than five days to a new medical session, in this opportunity it was only known according to its own words, that it would go to make a special treatment, that consisted of receiving several sessions of hyperbaric oxygenation.

However, before his departure in radio and television, he announced his plans and delegate his functions for the first time since he fell into disgrace. In this case he left the country in the hands of his vice-president for the time Tomas Dabajuro, and also asked the entire population of the country, if in a supposed denied, he did not return from the island, give the vote to Dabajuro so that He could continue with the work that had begun so many years ago.

Would that thought have been aloud around his feeling of aggression towards the people of the South American country his death sentence? Would Dabajuro's presence have been the cause of the Commander's physical disappearance? Only fate would reveal what had happened to President 'Galactico'.

Last minute news breakthrough': "President Lugo Galvez Riaz, has successfully emerged from the operation to which he was subjected, and is in a difficult post-operative process, so that the people can be calm," was the news matrix that was revealed on national television for the country and the world.

It was the first news that was officially available, in the voice of the President in charge, Tomas Dabajuro, who transmitted the information with the voice between cut, for the emotion that meant knowing that the president had already overcome this last moment surgical intervention.

"Commander you have to heal yourself, you have to return your people here it's waiting for you", those words pronounced by Dabajuro closed the chain transmission, which had been made to give information to the people, and also to the media of the world, which clamored for greater clarity about the situation of the President.

The following days were heavy in the national environment, and despite the fact that Christmas was the group that supported the government's management, it remained in expectation of the outcome. While those who opposed the regime, and those who knew the path that the country had taken, were attentive, because the disappearance of the President would represent an opportunity for change. However, they never adopted an attitude of disrespect before the pain of others and that is why silence was sepulchral throughout the national territory.

"Rodolfo! has leaked information that assures that President Lugo Galvez died last December 28th", Amilcar was heard giving information about the death of the President.
"But how is it possible if just a few minutes ago the Minister of Information and Communication, came out on national Radio and Television giving a report on the evolution of the President. In fact, a government commission would be traveling to the island with some documents that the president must sign, with some orders, laws, decrees," Rodolfo responded to Amilcar's adventure of saying that the president had died.

But the suspicion of Rodolfo and the media was activated. The fact of the trip to the Island to sign documents, decrees and laws was very strange. Why not wait for his recovery? Why that group trip to the Island to sign decrees and laws, when there is a national constitution that has the legal protocols for this type of facts? The situation was very strange because Amilcar's leaked information had grounds.

On March 5, 2013, on a national chain, members of the government cabinet, with a disjointed countenance, and weighing on the voice of their interlocutor, the death of the President of the South American Republic, Lugo Nataniel Galvez Riaz, was announced.

"At this moment I am fulfilling the most difficult mission of my life. And it's none other than to tell you that our beloved President has departed physically. His body has gone but not his spirit will remains among us. Galvez Lives, the Homeland goes on". Those would be the words of farewell that the in charge President Tomas Dabajuro and the cabinet of government gave to the eternal commander, with which a cycle was closed, perhaps the 'twist' that the Valastro brothers needed to finish their masterpiece, and to give step to the continental expansion of the communist project in the hemisphere.

With the death of President Lugo Galvez, there would be many changes in the direction of the Revolution, the country, and its people, including the main actors of the play that had been staged for two decades.

With Galvez's death Galvism died, a stream of people who followed the ideas of a man who according to most had no thought of his own, or at least was truncated by his handler from the Caribbean Island, so it was not a doctrine of thought. A man who was always manipulated by the masters of the hemisphere's leftist plot. That stream of people was left to the garete like cascade water with no direction other than the fall.

Only brilliant minds could keep alive the memory of Barinas' charismatic man, and those were the minds of the Valastro brothers. All to go beyond Communism in search of dominating the hemisphere, to become looters of a nation and territory that had been orphaned. Doubt still lurked in the thoughts of those who loved Galvez.

The masters of the parody, of the closing chapter wanted to handle the theory of blaming the Empire for the departure of the Giant, but many knew that the person responsible for the departure of the beloved President was near, in the environment, and was someone who knew that the Barines facing the death had stopped the bridles of that runaway animal that destroyed everything in its path. Only that it was late, he himself was inside the jaws of the monster that he helped to create, and simply it would not be needed any more. It was time to continue with the next phase of the conquest, with someone formed by them, someone who did not have the slightest hint of honesty, someone with nothing but emptiness within him, and the designated one was he, someone called Tomas Dabajuro.

The funerals of one of the most recognized figures of America in recent times, were going to be of the highest bill. But whose funerals?

The investigations carried out by the international press left many doubts and judging by events that took place during the funeral acts, there were enormous questions about what was inside the coffin that was exhibited in the Capital of the South American Republic, and to which thousands of followers had approached for seeing charming military coup plotter. The doubts grew and the reactions of the dignitaries were eloquent, to the point that the President of the land of Tango, had a frightening reaction to then look around and withdraw.

The public rumored that inside the coffin there was a wax puppet. Why photographic and video cameras were prohibited, and this increased the reactions and comments that were woven around that aberrant fact, which gave greater validity to the theory that had been handled for weeks, and was the one related to the fact that Lugo Galvez had died in the island approximately 2 months ago, that is to say before the end of 2012.

This was decisive, because from then on, everything that Galves theoretically would have signed on his deathbed was false, and would have no validity. From multimillion dollar loans granted by the Republic of Pina, to shipments of weapons and other items sent by Kursia. In theory both nations had been swindled.

Only one element would rescue the nation from any future claim on this matter, and that was the fact of the denunciations that were made publicly about the suspicions of the death of the President and about which those countries could not claim anything if it came to prove that the death of the galactic had taken place on the Island that December 2012 days after his last surgical intervention, from which it is suspected the President would have left without conscience, and only clung to life through medical equipments.

"Tomas remember that there are many doubts about your nationality and my idea could help us. I born in this country, I could grant you nationality if the case arises. The important thing is to create another pillar where to base everything in the event that it was known that you are of the sister Republic", said directly Lilia Sores.

"We must also give the impression of union, we must marry and give solidity to the process. It's like making two representatives close to Galvez, one stronger. That will allow us to face everything in a better way that will be our argument" continued Lilia Sores without detours, to which Dabajuro replied, "You are right Lilia but I do not know if it's the best moment, the people believe that just a few months ago the Commander left, and it would not look good," replied the heir.

But that's not how things were. The one in charge was the warrior, the lawyer, the same one who took out the Lieutenant Colonel from the Sare Prison, back in 1994, the one who faced everything when the coup plotter was a stranger in captivity, and now after the death of that figure, she could not be left out in the distribution of the booty. Thus things were done as she wished and preparations began for the assumption of Mrs. Lilia Sores, to her new role within the Revolutionary Government, nothing more and nothing less than the 'First Combatant'.

Everything was going good, the barrel of oil remained at over 100 dollars, a situation that allowed them to sustain themselves. The 'Chess twist' had taken place in spite of the setbacks that had occurred with the suspicions of the international press, even detecting 2 coffers, one arriving from Cuba with the decomposed body of the President, which for the urgency and the nerves had not been able to be embalmed. and the other with the wax puppet, which rests in the Cerro barracks, and to which they pay tribute permanently to make the people believe that there is Lugo Galvez body.

The money that entered by concept of the oil rent everything disappeared, as if by magic. One part was going to give to ghost projects that were never carried out, among others those planned by the carioca company Odebret and another good slice went directly to the pockets of a score allied nations, as payment for their services around to support with their votes any type of consultation about the precarious situation in the South American Republic.

Considering that the one who kept control of the band had passed away, each one began to carry out personal activities using the quota of power they had reached in the Government, and so it was as for example in the south of the country, the exploitation of gold began in a delinquent manner to favor characters from the Government and the Military assigned to the zone.

The situation became so complicated that massacres were carried out in the south of the country, in the fight for control of the gold mafia and the ecological damage would bring unimaginable consequences to the environment, even provoking landslides and seismic movements due to the alteration of the environment. Flora and fauna no longer existed in the south of the country, or at least what was left was in clear deterioration. They had de-boned the legend of 'El Dorado' and the military were involved in these events that showed that the current situation in the Bolivarian Republic went beyond Communism.

On the other hand the extraction of Uranium, which was sent to Chirán, there was a leak of Diamonds towards the Republic of Kutú, and the Coltan and Terum illegally extracted and taken to the Republic of Tirón.

The disaster and murder of ecology was something never before seen by mankind. Entire hectares of forest were destroyed, even the causes of the rivers that fed the largest dam of the southern cone were diverted, with the aim of reaching the legend of Gold, which turned out to be true, and despite the calamities of the population that began to suffer until the lack of water, in a country with the largest water resources of the southern cone.

"Amilcar, brother has happened something terrible. Do you remember the Doctor Juan Rafael Martinez of the city of Miami", said Rodolfo to Amilcar at the same time that he said to him, "Yes to whom I went to interview just a few months ago! He has just been found dead in his office, apparently as a result of cardiac arrest," concluded Rodolfo.

"I can't believe you, Rodolfo, if this guy could suffer from anything but his heart? , and working inside a hospital! and in Miami, no brother there happened something," said Amilcar, to which Rodolfo responded, "I also believe that bro, that guy was murdered. It's inconceivable that, being a doctor, he did not determine that he had a heart defect, and if so, how could they not react if he worked inside the most famous Hospital of that great Capital as Miami is".

The theory of Dr. Martinez's murder was meaningless at the time and sounded more like natural death than a plot. But as the two friends began to put their heads together, and to pose conjectures, they realized that it was not so far-fetched, and if it were so, Rodolfo would also be in danger, because he was one of the last to interview the man about the case of President Galvez.

"Rinnnnnnggg....ringggg", Rodolfo's phone rang at that very moment, and the number on screen was unknown. When he answered from the other side no one spoke.... "Yes, who is...hello..." and no one answered even when the call was open. Suddenly Rodolfo felt a deep, distant voice saying, 'You lost',

And then the call was hung up. Rodolfo looked at Amilcar and he was white as a piece of paper.

"Rodolfo and now that we do, you are in danger," said Amilcar, and Rodolfo replied to him, "No...I am not...we are in danger that is not the same.

The call had left them unarmed, especially because at that moment they were in the capital, the most complicated city in the South American country, and they would be easy prey.

"If we go to the Province, it would be less feasible for them to find us there at least for a while," Rodolfo said, seeking support from his friend.

"God Rodolfo I knew that share so many time with you, will complicate mi life". Amilcar almost cried.

At the end they calmed down, they leave the place where they were and went to Colonel Antonio Herrera's house, who was having a strong week with the events that were taking place. At this point, everyone distrusted everyone, and that was the main objective of the island's F3, the communist espionage group since the days of Commander Joel's arrival in power, and whose raison d'être was to evolve in the field of counter-intelligence, mass control and psychology of communication.

Those were their tools, even though eventually, when the occasion warranted it, they also tuse the weapons, remembering the times of the Union of Socialist Countries.

Possibly the F3 won't do anything, but they had already fulfilled their task by tormenting the last journalist who speak with the Famous Doctor Martinez. The point was that it was suspected that Martinez had revealed to Rodolfo some of the names he had as his source, since the person who passed the reports to him was one of the doctor's team members who attended to the late President Galvez and in such cases they do not usually leave loose ends, he, Rodolfo, was truly in danger, until at least he left the country.

"Chela answered me please, I have left you 3 messages", Rodolfo was heard to leave a fourth message in the voice mail of Chela, his friend of the Travel Agency, and it's that he had to use it in this occasion more than ever, for not leaving any type of trace in relation to the purchase of a ticket to leave the country. She calmed down and let a few minutes go by, when suddenly the phone rang and he felt his stomach spinning. With fear he approached the phone but when he saw Chela's picture on the screen, he quickly answered.

"Hello Chelita. How are you?", Rodolfo spoke politely but at the same time denoted anxiety. Chela greeted with the same courtesy but in the background she was missed by Rodolfo's rhythm.

"Chela, I need to get out of the country urgently, but I need you to buy the ticket," she said plainly through the headset.

"Rodolfo, are you all right?" asked Chela cautiously, to which Rodolfo replied apologizing. He was losing control and it wasn't good for anyone.

"Chela later I will explain to you, I'm in trouble, and I don't want to use my card, because I don't want it to be tracked," Rodolfo explained.

"Don't worry, Rodolfo, you can always count on me. Where do you want to go and with which line," asked Chela.

"Buy me something for Miami as soon as possible for the line you want," said Rodolfo.

"Look for the electronic ticket in your mail in the morning, it will be there with the itinerary," said her friend.

"Thank you Chela, thank you a lot, you don't know what you just did," he said goodbye with a kiss across the line and Rodolfo immediately turned off his smartphone.

Chela really didn't know what she had just done, she had gotten into trouble, but she wouldn't know until later.

As a result of the surrender of the Ministries of Identification and Foreigners to the agents of the Island, all the control of issuance of ID cards and Passports was in charge of the Regime that made all the arrangements from outside. This was the reason why governments from different parts of the world, constantly detained citizens of the Middle East, in ports and airports who did not have a Latin American appearance, did not even speak Spanish, but had passports from the South American Republic.

This fact even created several international conflicts all the time, that came to stop and capture terrorists trying to enter different countries of Europe with the Passports granted by the Revolutionary Government, obviously with the approval of the Valastro brothers.

In this sense, Rodolfo knew that he would not be safe anywhere because the tentacles of that network reached several corners of the world and the proof was the strange death of Doctor Juan Rafael Martinez, product perhaps of what he knew and his contacts with the Island.

While these facts complicated the life of the journalist Rodolfo Vega and his environment as a result of his investigations, in the country the date of the new elections was slowly approaching, through which the successor to the Presidency of the late Lugo Nataniel Galvez Riaz would be officially elected.

The sovereign was clear about what was happening and for this reason the society as a whole, students, guilds, farmers, businessmen and political parties, were forming a single block to expel the government which since 1999 had handed over the country to foreign entities.

The Campaign for the elections began then with a peculiar slogan: 'Galvez vive, la Patria sigue' (Galvez lives, the Homeland follows), which lasted only 10 days according to the regulations as known from the CEE. But this was more because of the haste to finish the 'Enrosque', before any possibility that the truth about the date of Galvez's death appeared, or the birth certificate of the Candidate Tomas Dabajuro, of whom it was certain but without proof, that he had been born out of the national territory.

He had begun the fateful journey in which Dabajuro could perpetuate himself in power. Like always the Island's instructions were to go to vote late as usual to set the trap. The regime publicly shouted that the people would vote early, so that the collectives could operate during the first part of the day without margins of error and assaulting whoever was voting. Then after 5 p.m. the government adept groups would come out to show that there were a lot of people and muscle as to the followers supporting the communist project.

At night there were still followers of the 21st Century Revolution at the voting tables, while the information traveled in real time to the Situation Room on the Island, from where they executed the adjustments by region and returned them to the CEE counting room, in order to have everything at hand and announce in the shortest possible time after the closing of the tables, the new victory of the current President in charge, who by the way never separated himself from the position as indicated by the law and the constitution. The people suspected and even intuited that the majority had voted for a change, a consequence of the fatigue of the population due to the excesses that had begun to come to light.

The most notorious part of the infamous day was when Yurislay Orejuela, with a happy face and the coldness of those who are full of emptiness, announced the victory and re-election of the candidate of the Government Tomas Dabajuro, a moment in which the people began to go out into the street to set fire to the regional and central headquarters of the electoral Commission, due to the shameless robbery to which had been subjected the population. The fraud carried out by the Government and by the electronic voting system had been too evident and the people were not willing to let them get away with it from the Island.

At that time the Government was beginning to take the army out into the streets to attack the population, through the disproportionate use of force, with the National Guard, and the State Police, in addition to the collision groups called collectives that since the beginning of the revolutionary process had protected the Government in an underhand manner but with all their permission. In the midst of the chaos that was being created, the representatives of the regime immediately placed the opposition candidate, and with threats of extermination, forced the candidate to ask the citizens to return home, one more time.

To the astonishment of many the instructions from the Campaign command of the election winner were that the people would go home to sound pots and pans.

This was the straw that spilled the glass in a day that could end the silent invasion, but the pressure and threats of the government on the political factors in turn, were so great that the political group of the opposition candidate had to accept defeat. In the following days, they would become aware of the serious error committed, and began to denounce the fraud at the level of international organizations, which had allowed them to grant the victory to the representative of the communists of the island.

Those denunciations made in international courts, were what in a certain way put chain to the beasts represented by the Republic of Pina and Kursia, since they were only waiting for this process to continue the shameless plundering of wealth in exchange for trifles. The warnings of those responsible for the Opposition were eloquent and well-toned. One related to the Nationality of the virtual winner of the fraud, who was said to be a foreigner. The second most intoned chorus related to the date of the Commander's death, a theory that came to life. And the third had to do with documented evidence of electoral fraud, including optical cable.

Marina Bartolomeo, was a warrior woman. Besides being beautiful, a common characteristic of the women of the South American Republic, she possessed a mixture between the attractiveness of the Caribbean and the fineness of the European woman. Studied, active and always given to help others.

Marina was one of the many Venezuelan women who gave herself that year 2014, in which young students from all over the country said enough to so many atrocities, and after three emblematic events always linked to the insecurity and precarious situations of the country, initiated protests and demands to the government in different regions of the country.

The first one in going out to protest was the 'Andino State', from which several Presidents of the South American Republic have emerged, whose trigger was the murder of a student at the hands of the underworld. The young people decided to go out with everything to protest against so much harassment until the people unite them in an unprecedented gesture because as true warriors they literally blocked the State.

Given the general situation of the country, which was close to chaos, the students of the capital city joined the protests, putting in check the incipient and useless government of Tomas Dabajuro, who did nothing but flatter the management of Lugo Galvez, who by the way was close to completing the first year of death, and still followed the chronic discourse, such as the one that has nothing to do or say. But if there was much to do, like to develop a country, rich in natural and human resources which was anxious to get out of the lethargy.

Marina was one of the many mothers who had lost a child killed by the government, in the first round of protests of that quarter of 2014, Marina was torn apart because her son in the university studies phase had been murdered by one of the henchmen of Dabajuro's regime, who apparently was going to surpass his teacher Joel Valastro as to the cruelty used in order to remain in power.

"The National Guards who murdered my son are from the Island, I listened their accent....If it is possible...If it is possible," Marina shouted on the loudspeaker over and over again, during a march heading to the headquarters of the courts of the 'Andino State'. The march grew in number of participants, in heart, in energy, and this alerted the henchmen of the Government, which had become Dictatorial regime, from the moment in which they began the massacre against the students.

"Let's fight for our country, it's time, we can't allow more abuses of foreigners in our nation", shouted Robinson, another of the leading students, who was the President of the Los Andes University's Student Center. "I call on society as a whole, on businessmen, on State agencies to stop this situation that kills our population and makes us hostages in our land of foreign henchmen", words that Robinson Collantes offered to the masses through loudspeakers, but which were repeated again and again by those who firmly continued the protest for freedom.

At that moment, shots began to be heard, in the middle of the march, just as groups of motorists approached and practically burned clothes and shot the students leading the protest in the front. The students then reacted with blunt objects, defending themselves from the aggression to which they had been subjected.

"One of the many citizens, father of one of the hearts of the future of that beautiful land, shouted, "Quickly an ambulance, those cursed ones are killing our boys.
"Help...help....here....I grabbed one of the shooters", shouted Jesus another one of the students who had experience in Martial Arts, reason why he was able to knock down some of the motorized ones, keeping him as hostage.

The confusion in the environment was disappearing, to give way suddenly to anger and helplessness that were in turn becoming the reality that plagued the people. After several minutes, after hitting the hostage enough, they would tie him to a public lighting post totally naked, to exemplify that in the march there were no murderers.

At that point, at the other side of street fortunately medical units of the entities responsible for the health sector were adhered to the march, and therefore the ambulances would help to anyone who needed it, as indeed happened. Only one of the students had lost his life, with a point-blank shot to the head, an unequivocal sign that the executor was a foreign mercenary, probably from the Island.

While this was happening in the 'Andina region', protests were multiplying in the West of the Republic. One in the central part of the city, another in the sector known as Hermosa Vista, in which there were confrontations between young people fighting with cardboard shields, against foreign henchmen accompanied by some native troops of the country.

In the main highway, the gateway to the west of the country, the people were protesting and preparing to reach the main bridge in the region, which is an emblem of the people of the area. After having advanced approximately one hundred meters, they were ambushed by Agents of the Police of the municipality in whose territory was the emblematic bridge. With shoots from a distance, there were gunshot wounds.

"I'm Father Altar, and demand that the authorities of the municipality stop the fire because this march is peaceful", through the loudspeakers the words of the priest guiding the march were heard, when a Television camera could see how a shot grazed the shoulder of the priest and fell to the ground. At that moment the crowd was in help of the religious, but in the other side of the street a young man had been shot in the leg, moment in which the aggressors imprisoned by panic receded without losing sight of enraged mass, only detained by the fear instilled by the 'irons' carried by the cowardly agents of the regime.

The media took each scene in photo and video, but only a camera could capture the moment of the impact, against the young man wounded in the leg, an image that immediately went around the world to leave evidence of the atrocities that were committing for the dictatorship against the population of the country.

After this, the journalists and cameramen of the different media began to receive threats, especially those who by misfortune and fulfilling their duty, captured just the moment of the bullet impact.

From then on, their lifes would be ruined, as they were persecuted and harassed until they had to flee the country.

The Capital was a pandemonium, the protests grew and slowly they were joining one with another, until reaching massive levels. The tanks of the State organisms, called Metropolis Police, as well as of the National Guard, went around assaulting the population, to intimidate and assassinate any case. Not to mention the Tanqueta called the 'Whale' which with the force of water pressure moved the citizens like paper tokens and pushed them at great speed against the walls or trees.

The level of evil was not normal, the henchmen of the Dictatorship entered the residences, knocking down the gates without any reason, and with the regulatory armament they broke the windows of the vehicles, the guard posts, threw grenades to destroy everything in their path. The only objective was to instill terror, like an armed confrontation in the Middle East.

The people insisted to say, neither the physicist of each mercenary, nor the way of speaking, nor the execution of their deeds identified them as agents of the country. Without a doubt they were trained personnel sent at that moment to contain the people and avoid the fall of the Dictatorship.

Those who attacked were mercenaries brought from other latitudes to assassinate and avoid losing the jewel of the crown, which was really what the South American Republic meant, speaking in terms of leadership, wealth and geographical position, and taking into consideration that in the island called the Pearl of the Caribbean, the presence of a terrorist cell had been proven, just as there was another in the southern cone in the triple common border.

For the invading band it was unacceptable to lose the South American Republic.

A leader, whom the Government feared, was present at the convocation of the people. A leader heir to the Bolivar caste, who courageously guided the students and the people in claiming their rights.

With a loudspeaker in hand he motivated the feat, when on the day of youth the people vibrated, the voice of Leonardo Volpez was heard firmly.

"Boys, today on this day full of light, we must show the world what we are capable of. Let us peacefully ask for our rights to be respected. The government cannot run over us and at the same time unilaterally demand that we citizens be like lambs. The people of Venezuela, represented by us, deserve freedom and security. It deserves a better future, for us and for our children!", and in every breath of air Volpez took, he transmitted a gale of energy to that legion of young people watered by the streets of the South American country, like leaves in autumn he had an oak tree in his environment.

It was then that the government understood that it had to stop that source of inspiration, a gale, that breath of strong wind that made the foundations of the Dictatorship move with fury.

And the deception made an act of presence in the person of Diogenes Capelli, the same one who made his apparitions from nothing, as if obscuring everything when he looked. Already the leader of the Revolution, Lugo Galvez, had set him aside as corrupt, as if he were a shadow full of emptiness.
Now at a time when demons were being liberated beyond communism, he had been strengthened as fed by the evil unleashed in the country, and taking advantage of that moment he imprisoned the genuine leader, under the pretext that he was

going to be assassinated to hold the government responsible for his disappearance.

Nothing could be more false than that theory, which would lead Leonardo Volpez to be the most precious hostage and through whom the dictatorship would take control of the nation's streets.

That fact, plus the dictatorial decision to turn off the two most important television screens that were transmitting internationally the realities of what was happening, throughout the national territory as were the Channel of the sister Republic and the Channel of the States Together. This stabilized the regime again to start an attack in the neighborhoods of the country, stopping groups of Venezuelans who claiming their rights had altered the tranquility of the dictatorship.

Finally, after once again staining the streets with the blood of the people and violating human rights through operations called OLP, Operation to Liquidate the People, as reflected in their various NGO reports, began the onslaught of the regime kidnapping, imprisoning, torturing and sometimes disappearing civilians and military in every corner of the national geography. The regime led by Tomas Dabajuro managed to retake the helm of his perverse journey.

 But....until when?

"We can't go on stage yet, that could ruin our plans to liberate the Homeland," said Colonel Antonio Herrera seeing the facts through the media, more through social networks than by any other means, at the same time that he hit the table with frustration when he saw how the evil one of the Island ordered the murder of Bolivar's children.

"At some point, divine providence would take over the black of your soul," said the Colonel again and again, to the point of losing the perspectives of the meeting they were beginning.

However, they had to quickly coordinate the actions to be taken, because once the regime was naked around the issue of human rights, the reaction of the democratic sector of the Armed Forces became more viable.

"Gentlemen, every time the individual who calls himself President of the South American nation acts, he gives us more room for action and opens the crack through which we can hunt him down.

The line that divides defending the constitution or carrying out a coup d'état is extremely thin, and we must be firm and sure of the steps we take. We cannot afford to cross the line because we would be punished by history," shouted Colonel Herrera, who was addressing a select group of soldiers. At that moment one of the youngest leaders entered the scene, a Captain whose words echoed the thoughts of those present...

"But neither can we stand by and watch as a group of thugs disrupt the Republic more than they have broken it so far". It was the words of the pilot Omar Lares, a super trained Commissioner of the State Security Corps, who had become a key piece of dissidence, the product of everything he had seen, and also the product of the murder of one of his brothers at the hands of the underworld.

From now on, the meetings of those who opposed the government were going to be with unknown location until the last minute, not even Amilcar, who was close to Colonel Herrera and with the confidence he had earned was allowed to attend that meeting. As for Rodolfo, who was missed by some of the attendees, official information was given that he had to leave the country for security reasons, since he was a marked target.

Taking advantage of his experience within the Force, Rodolfo had described the position of the military. This position had been expressed in a letter he had sent via e-mail to his action group. The situation of the military personnel was difficult, as the F3 Isleño had mutated and had become an excellent hunting group of loyal officers of the population. They had evolved to such an extent that they had infiltrators in all strata of the Forces.

the money that came in for oil rent was so brutal that the commissions that they gave for information on dissidence allowed the families of that informers to live comfortably anywhere in the world, even in the second generation. In such a way that this could only be fought with honorability. That is to say that those who belonged to the elite gathered in that instance were the true patriots heirs of Bolivar.

One of the great advantages that existed was that the corrupt Generals were fully identified, not only by the internal intelligence of the group, but also by the North American intelligence, which had called to this group 'The Cartel of the Suns', due to their proven participation in gigantic shipments of drugs to the United States and Europe.

The plan of that platform that sought to conquer the American hemisphere, was to destroy societies in their young segments just as the British Crown did in the 17th century when it invaded some territories and tried to take over others, through the legalization of opium and based on the Narcoeconomy that destroyed societies as, for example, it almost did with China in order to achieve its objectives.

At this point the strategic alliance maintained by the regime of the South American Republic with the FAR was key, since it was the main supplier of the drug that was sent to the destinies already described, with the firm purpose of destroying the youth of the most powerful countries in the world, to then try to penetrate by that way in the heart of each one of those societies.

Behind the invasion that the Island was concretizing to the South American nation, there was more. There were plans for the expansion of Communism throughout the hemisphere, and even plans for world destabilization, through protests for the rights of minorities, speaking in religious terms, race and gender. In this aspect came into play powerful groups and millionaires, who caused any kind of disturbance of public order as marches or protests, thus changing the pace of nations and therefore lowering the stock value of their main industries and institutions, and when this happened immediately bought those shares to then stabilize and sell when they were on the rise.

Some of these minds had names and surnames, and one of them was the world-renowned philanthropist Juvenal Moros, who sheltered behind a network of charitable foundations. In this way at the end of the road was completely clean and without any kind of stain in its history.

While the military were looking for a point of guarantee to act and dismantle the plague that loot the nation every day, falsely protected in the constitution of the Republic, the parliamentary elections were prepared, perhaps the last to be held under the current scheme of free election and direct suffrage.

2015 would be the decisive year to retake the Legislative Power in which little by little spaces had been gained, since in comparison with the year 2005, in which the opposition abandoned the elections due to lack of guarantees, the 2010 elections had already taken up seats and this in a certain way prevented many of the aberrations attempted by the group representing the Government of the Island.
But history was going to change and the democracy was going to arrive at least to the Parliament.

And how could this have happened?

"I want to introduce you to Rodolfo Vega, a journalist who has had to flee abroad, due to the constant harassment and threats that the Dictatorship is making to Communication Professionals, precisely to prevent them from spreading to the world the truth of what is happening in the nation. In addition, Rodolfo has useful information regarding a character who altered the software used by Transmatic since 2006. In this way Jesus Troncone made the corresponding introduction of Rodolfo in the working group that would try to help the liberation of Venezuela from abroad.

Jesus Troncone, was a Computer Engineer, who had become an eminence in his area. This gave him credentials to ensure that the election processes in the South American nation had been controlled by software to alter the processes and thus the results. Under this premise, a group of experts was formed, which was later expanded to include Rodolfo Vega in the area of communications. This expansion was intended to strengthen with trained personnel the project that was called 'Blocking Fraud'.

"Rodolfo thank you for agreeing to be part of our team," said Troncone while giving him a handshake.

"Where are you from, Rodolfo," asked the engineer.

"I'm from the Province of the country," answered Rodolfo asking, "And where are you from? To what Jesus replied, "I am from the Capital, chamo", and laughing they went to eat something in the cafeteria next door.

The project or plan consisted of providing support and guidance to a group of computer scientists who would be in the South American Republic on Election Day, to try to prevent the government from would execute its fraud plan.

This was going to be uphill, taking into consideration the electrical energy problems that existed in the country, and also the constant hunt that the henchmen of the regime had against any site where they detected computer activity via the Internet.

The Government's computer scientists, placed there with orders from the Island, have as much or more experience and tools than the own experts in computer science that are watered by the world, in this case they could easily engage any challenge to the knowledge with the best in the technological area.

"Rodolfo look unfortunately we have aborted everything we are doing and we will be calling you if we change our mind," was heard from the other side of the line and then he felt how the communication was closed.

Rodolfo was worried about what had happened and it wouldn't be until a week later when Jesus Troncone called him again and asked him if they could have a cup of coffee, to which Rodolfo gave his acceptance. They agreed on a time and place and went to meet.

"Hello Rodolfo, I honestly feel sorry for what happened. We didn't really expect this to happen, but it did. I hope you can excuse us, because the situation was complicated, we detected an infiltrated person and that destroyed the project that was mounted, so 'officially' nothing will be done", Jesus told him exactly what happened while moving his head from one side to the other as a sign of frustration, pressing his lips as he regretted having expanded the group, because it was at that moment, when an infiltrated got in.

Rodolfo who always wanted to walk faster asked him if he could know who was the person, for taking care about, since he had fled the country because of the harassment and direct threats of the regime and should be cautious or would have to leave that city so frequented by files of the dictatorship.
Jesus told him, "Rodolfo do not worry that the guy came out as a cork cover of the country because it was denounced to Federal agencies, and that file will not hurt.

"Rodolfo what if I wanted to ask you 'unofficially'," Jesus talk almost whispering, "Would you be interested in following our plan with a smaller group," said Jesus raising an eyebrow in approval sign. Rodolfo replied, "Of course Jesus, there was no need, I'll sign up one more time.

That's how the small group got down to work, changed meeting places, changed cell phones, and agreed not to give the number to anyone but those involved. They changed meeting places, and never repeated a venue. It was also reported where it was going to be at the last minute practically 10 minutes before each meeting and that was how they managed to meet the objectives regarding the first phase of the plan which was to discover precisely how the trap was to be able to combat and block the fraud that was suffering the people of the South American nation.

The crisis in the country was growing every day, and still with oil at approximately 100 dollars a barrel. This situation caught the attention and the common people wondered where the oil rent money was. It had already been known by the mouth of the deceased President Lugo Galvez, that the budgets of the last years had been calculated at the rate of 60 dollars a barrel, and that the surplus went to Fondo Unico, whose control he alone had.

That was so and no one knew where the surplus was, but and the $60 a barrel where they were. Everything was deteriorating, the hospitals, the transportation systems, the national electrical system, and no one knew where the money was.

To the Government's disgrace, recently the investigation portal 'Interleaks' had publicly disclosed some e-mails and information of international frauds where some names of personalities of the

South American nation's government appeared and their relation with millionaire accounts in tax havens, that was a misfortune for the gang of malefactors that in bad time invaded the country.

It is there when a group of recognized politicians who could win the next parliamentary elections begin to go, to different tax havens, such as Switzerland, Andorra, the Cayman Islands, in short, the destinations where capitals are hidden, and that is when they discover the pot of life. Millions upon millions were deposited in the accounts of relatives and frontmen of the different members of the Dictatorship because at this point and after uncovering that pot, this group could be classified as a real dictatorship.

Customary revision. Tuned Transmatic Machines. Witnesses of table totally with instructions. Media with limited access to polling stations. Collectives stationed around polling stations. Optical cable in perfect state of transmission. "President magazine concluded everything in order and under control," said psychiatrist George Ortiguez to Tomas Dabajuro, as if trying to give him peace of mind knowing that under normal conditions and without fraud the defeat for the government would have been monstrous.

Only the lifeline that the optical cable had become could either avoid defeat or at least make it less humiliating, should the country become a disaster as had already occurred in 2013. In general terms, the Parliamentary elections still did not have the strength to remove the Band from power, the same that they had obtained and remained at 'any cost', as the government's campaign slogan said, source of inspiration for the collectives and armed gangs that the government maintained economically.

When the date of the event arrived, the people voted massively and due to the delay caused by the electoral bodies, the people did not leave the voting centers. On the contrary, this situation seemed to motivate people more than in groups and in order to protect each other, they went to vote. It was noticeable in the intention of the vote that the people wanted a change that had been elusive, and it was not for lack of desires, it was because of the macabre game that had mounted the government through the electoral committee.

The day passed with difficulty. The operative or plan of the State to guarantee the votes, was failing, obviously with all intention. The government was doing the impossible so that the people would get tired, so that every citizen would go home to play dominoes and watch Television, but in the queues the citizens continued despite the fact that serious incidents such as threats and even collective harming the people occurred. In the capital, for example, in one of the best-known parishes, a band of collectives shot into the queues, leaving a dead person in the balance.

The population towards a supreme effort. It was left out in the vicinity of the voting centers taking care of the process, since the citizens knew the customs of the Government.
But ????????
Shortly before the closing time of the tables there was an incident that left the technicians in the counting and totalization room in place, and this was the loss of computer contact with the Situation Room of the Island, a situation that caused alarm in the Government, in the electoral body and in the Amana, Capital of the Island where they were literally hitting the walls for not being able to re-establish the lost contact.

To all these the time advanced and obligatorily the technicians of the Totalizaron Room had to execute their work which was to make the real count, as they had always done. The point was that on this occasion they could not send the totals to the Island for readjustment and subsequent resending back for announcement and that literally killed them.

After a few minutes and the nervousness shown by the Chief Rector of the CEE, Yurislay Orejuela, she had no choice but to announce the results adjusted to the truth, that is, the announcement of a resounding victory of the People over the Valastro/Communist Dictatorship that was established in the South American nation.

"With a result of 112 opposition deputies and 55 Officialists, the results of the 2015 parliamentary elections are closed", and babbling was the only thing that the maximum representative of the Revolution could do, who saw with terror how the Legislative Power was taken away from them in front the eyes of the world, with an absolute majority. Then there would come some tantrums to prevent the oath of a group of deputies in order to avoid that absolute majority that could destroy what in 20 years it had cost the Dictatorship to create.

The recovery of Democracy was in sight, while the streets overflowed with festivities, always in a restrained manner as a result of the terror that the collectives had installed in every centimeter of the national territory.

Immediately one of the most corrupt members of the regime, Diogenes Capelli, made a call to the followers of the Government not to be defeated by this error in the count, and asked the collectives to go out and defend the victory. To this quickly and without any other option, the Minister of Defense replied. "Regretting it very much the results are final, and the opposition to won the National Assembly", the Minister concluded his intervention and acted intelligently, since if the people exploited by some attempt to change the results, they would not only have lost the National Assembly, but also they could have lost power.

This result was unexpected for the members of the Government gang, so they ran and immediately called for meetings and direct contact with the Island to find out what had happened and to try to minimize the collateral damage caused by having lost the Legislative Power.

In this way, in violation of the Constitution and all established laws, a group of judges is expressly sworn in before the end of the year to form a new Supreme Court of Justice, with death threats for the previous members, if it was the case that they did not accept their retirement or did not present their resignation. It was a film by Alfred Hitchcock what was being experienced the last days of the year in the nation.

Faced with the threats, the previous magistrates accepted what the members of the band cystated in the Government Palace said, and it was thus that before the end of the year they formed a new Maximum Court of Justice (TMJ), with incapable judges who did not comply with the regulations established by the Constitution. This new ilegal entity made up of members of the Revolution had a mission and was to neutralize or at least hinder the work of the recently elected Assembly of the South American Nation.

"Jesus we achieved it, we did it, we rescued the country, blocking the continuous fraud that those devils were doing", Rodolfo shouted constantly to all the members of the team, the joy was incredible since they had put their knowledge, acquired in their mother country, to the service of the Republic. Now they put the game upside down to the Dictatorship and would have to move their pieces very well to remain in power.

One of the first actions that the newly elected National Assembly had by absolute majority, was to request before the executive the immediate release of the political prisoners of those who warning the ideas of the revolution had supported the people.

Subsequent to that action, others came among which was the creation of a Commission to investigate the fate of national funds that were in the hands of the figurehead of the members of the Bolivarian Government.

It was like that as the deputy Tulio Montero had already gone a long way in tracking the location of the nation's capitals. Only missing the names of the people who, after a commercial firm or using a figurehead, that were on that list were still pending.
World banking and financial organizations could not give this missed information to natural or legal persons. They were only obliged to give it to governmental representations, and that could not be done before the National Assembly took office.

For this reason, once the new Assembly was sworn in, and just as the work commissions were designated, the legal process for requesting information from the international financial institutions was initiated.

Instructions were sent through the Legislative Power to the Banks of the Tax Havens mentioned above, and without objection they began to show everything.

The amount of money was so overwhelming that a calculator could not measure the economic damage done to the nation. The figure was over 4 Billion dollars. What really mattered was the prompt response of the financial and banking agencies, freezing funds instantly, and leaving the criminals who ruled the country penniless.

It was obligatory to recognize the enormous capacity and intelligence of those who held power, supported from all four angles by the military dome made up of the corrupt military, the smugglers and the members of the Cartel de los Soles.

The commission created by the dictatorship and headed by one of the leaders of the government, Diogenes Capelli, all this after losing the parliamentary elections and before the inauguration of the new National Assembly, would have the purpose of blocking all the laws and decisions emanating from the Legislative Palace.

However, one of the most transcendental events in the history of the South American nation, managed to be executed, and was no other than the swearing-in of the Tribunal Maximo de Justicia (TMJ) Legitimo, which would comply with the rules and laws, respecting the Constitution of the Republic, whose selection was made attached to the existing legal regulations in the country and complying with the protocols and times required by the Constitution of the Republic....

Once selected and sworn in, a persecution began on the part of the repressive organs of the dictatorship, against the magistrates, to the point that they had to flee, hide across the borders by land or take refuge in the embassies of democratic countries.

With this fact, the last vestige of democracy that could have remained in the country was detached, and the eyes of the world saw with astonishment how a group of bandits destroyed the foundations of the Republic.

"Colonel Julio, what are we going to do now in the midst of this disaster and this violation of the Constitution," asked Attorney General Yuliza Ortigoza Friaz, anxiously as time ran out.

"I don't know what to think at this moment, let me coordinate to see what tools we have and to whom we have, but if I am wrong they will not only go against you, they will also go against me," said Colonel Julio, a man of color who was known for his mettle when executing and defending decisions.

"I find no other way out than to help you leave the country, because the new National Constituent Assembly will be installed soon and after that they will remove both the National Assembly and the Attorney General of the Republic," he said anticipating what was going to happen, judging by the security with which I speak, those were the exact plans of the dictatorship.

"How could an organ created or invented by a gang of criminals destroy the Republic?," said the Prosecutor, while walking from one side to the other trying to give birth to ideas that would allow a margin of action supported by the law and the Constitution of the Republic.

The plans of the Dictatorship were to invent a popular consultation to give an end to the Republic, through the establishment of a National Constituent Assembly, which was to be, for the National Assembly (Legal), what the Maximum Court of justice created 'illegally' and in an express way, had been for the true Maximum Court of Justice (Legal).

"The bad news, Prosecutor, is that they will do it with the 'Transmatic' machines and use the optical cable connected to the Island," concluded Colonel Julio, while inviting the Prosecutor to move, since in the situation in which they found themselves they could not stay long in the same place because they would be located, marked and possibly eliminated, especially her who represented one of the powers that had decided to move away from the conspiracy.

On July 30, 2017, the Government transformed into Dictatorship mounted a unilateral process, which did not have the support of any of the powers legitimately formed, as the National Assembly and the Attorney General of the Republic, since that fact was a process that tried to make disappear the constitution of the South American Republic, which had been modified the giant Lugo Galvez, simply because this fact would allow the band to stay in power against all odds.

The day of the process was evident the rejection of people to see the streets absolutely empty. That day the CEE after sending data to the island, logically through the optical cable and then its respective return with adjustments made by experts, was prepared to give the results. Knowing the directors of the electoral organ, it was to be expected the success speech of the day that had just been fulfilled with the participation of the society vote. What nobody imagined was the impudence and the courage that the Dictatorship had when offering such a high number of participation, knowing that the social networks and the few means of communication that covered the event made it clear that nobody went out to vote by an absolutely illegal apparatus, whose only objective was to annul the decisions that on the legal matter, issued by the National Assembly.

When the directors of the electoral body revealed that the participation was above the 8 million votes, the whole world immediately pronounced itself in this respect, and counting only with 5 countries worldwide, the legality of that farce called the National Constituent Assembly, It was absolutely eliminated.

Immediately and as if to put the icing on the cake the company 'Transmatic', until that day in charge of conducting the electronic voting process and also had been doing since 2006, strongly denied this fraud, through a press conference international offered from the city of London, after its managers were safe guard outside the borders of the South American nation, more for the absurd than for anything else, knowing that the country had evidently been left empty streets throughout the day.

In that press conference was confirmed that the vote had barely exceeded 2 million votes, so they considered that the figure given by the electoral committee had been a scandalous fraud. These declarations of the company in charge of the process, finished taking off the elastic to a mask that for a long time was fallen, but now it was not before the people of the South American Republic, but before the eyes of the world.

By the force they installed themselves and achieved their mission which was to create an organ whose medium-term objective was to rewrite the National Constitution and adapt it to its invading project, even legalizing the plundering of the heritage of the nation that had operated for long time. There, in that constitution, there would be impunity for acts of corruption whose evidence had been handed over by the world's banks and financial systems to the legally elected National Assembly of the Republic.
At this point, the 'Express and Illegitimate Supreme Court' issued a decision by which it granted itself the functions of the National Assembly legally elected by the people last December.

"People of Venezuela through this press conference and through the attribution conferred on me by the Republic I declare that the constitutional thread has been broken, after the Illegal Maximum Court of Justice, took for itself, the legal functions of the Republic, exclusive competence of the AN", textually in a personal and courageous act the Attorney General of the South American Republic, Yuliza Ortigoza friaz, took for granted her position regarding the legal madness that this illegitimate Tribunal intended to make, by orders of the Island Regime.

"Doctor, the Illegitimate Assembly has just installed itself and appointed a new Attorney General, and they are about to issue an arrest warrant against you", Colonel Julio told the Attorney General, who was hurriedly gathering some belongings, to prepare to leave the country.

But how?

"How will we get out of Julio? we can't go to the airports," the prosecutor said nervously to the Colonel and he replied, "You can trust me, anyway at this point you don't have many options," he ended July while parking his personal use vehicle so as not to raise suspicions.

The departure of the Prosecutor of the South American Republic, had to be done by sending a decoy to the International Airport of the Capital, and another one to one of the cities of the interior. However, the escape which was also being made by the husband of the Prosecutor, was made by land through the border with the sister Republic, obviously with military accompaniment, otherwise it would have been impossible.

Immediately the Colonel left back, but the only problem was to arrive as soon as possible to the Capital of the Republic not to raise suspicions. When everything was under control, the Prosecutor asked for help from the authorities of the neighboring country, who, faced with the knowledge of what was happening after the border limit, gave all possible support to the legal Prosecutor of the South American Republic.

Only 24 hours passed when the Prosecutor from the Capital of the neighboring country called a press conference to denounce the facts and to swear before the memory of Bolivar that he was going to do his best to give back to the South Americans the country they were losing through the invasion of the regime of the

Island. Immediately after the journalists' conference he had offered, he met with representatives of the U.S. government, who were behind the track of the members of the Soles cartel; of its supposed leader, Deputy Diogenes Capelli, also of Nelson Revenga and another major brand official who was behind the granting of passports of the South American Republic, to members of terrorist groups from the Middle East who had already been detained in different airports around the world with passports issued by him and mounted by the island government.

More and more military deserters were leaving the country with evidence and information about crimes committed by the dictatorial regime of Venezuela. That situation reached such a point that after initiating investigations at the judicial level, the U.S. Government drew up several lists of officials to whom it applied sanctions, as it they were unable to justify the astronomical bank accounts and the assets they possessed, both in the name of family members and frontman.

And while, anarchy took over the streets of every city in the South American Republic, whether it was the lack of food or medicine, or the scarcity of gasoline that grew more and more every day and whose 'modus operandi' was to pass the transport trucks after the border, where the military the cost of each one was one dollar, turned it into 20 thousand dollars.

When it seemed that the legitimate National Assembly had everything under control, something hindered its free action. The calculation of the members of the regime was such that they planned future moves on their chessboard.

"Ignasio I don't know what to do, you know this morning one of the pro-government deputies approached me to ask me the time, like an excuse, and taking advantage of the fact that no one was around, he told me clear and abruptly that if I did not do that the government wanted, they were going to imprison my children and my nephews and nieces accusing them, of some contracts they were granted a couple of years ago around some electrical plants and electrical material, some of which were damaged. The truth is that they put me between a sword and a wall," Eny Ramos told Ignasio Garcia, another of the deputies of the opposition party.

"Eny and what are you going to do," Garcia asked.
"What am I going to do?, I told him that inform to his group that I was already aware and I asked them for time to lower the tone little by little, because I can not do this all at once. I asked them to

let me continue attacking at that level and in a progressive way I will lower my guard until I finish my term as president of the Chamber", and being more of a father than a politician, Eny Ramos ended his comment with Congressman Garcia.

The dictatorship had the Achilles heel of each one. And those deputies who didn't have a weak spot were simply invented by opening a file on them for whatever reason, they were imprisoned them and worn them out in the dungeons with tortures designed for that purpose.

The hunger in the streets was shameful for a country millionaire in natural resources, minerals, and above all in youth and human resources. But the plan was that, from the beginning, only that the loss of the parliamentary elections, forced to accelerate the march.

Both events slowed down in some way the hidden rhythm of his plan. Due to this the Band of delinquents decided to be more aggressive than ever, making use of the slogan that says that 'the best defense is the attack!'.

"Brother, my wife and my children are there, protected but I must return to get them out, without them I have no life here," Rodolfo said when he spoke to Amilcar, who kept him permanently informed of the plans to eliminate the dictatorship.

"And when would you come?" asked Amilcar, to which Rodolfo replied, "I don't have a date, my brother, but I'm not going to divulge that. First I coordinate everything, I prepare everything for the exit and then I report back to the group. If I needed help, I would let you know Amilcar, thank you brother", and with a bit of nerves both friends said goodbye through the telephone line.

The situation in the whole country was complicated and due this the military group was working hard. One moonless night, a vehicle approached the headquarters of the Paracay Barracks, one of the most important nationwide, and when the people got out of the vehicle......

"Stick there and don't talk, we need a guide to the bottom, to the vault", the leader of the group had captured the sentry and subjected him, when in one movement the sentry activated his firearm, more to warn the barracks, than to hit his captor, because his cannon had not reach him.

At that moment began an exchange of fire that did not cease for at least two hours. Fortunately for the intruders, the second in command of the group was able to subdue and guide the second sentry and he had taken them to the vault of the park of gunpowder weapons and tanks of war, the largest warehouse in the country, and the jewel of the Armed Forces.

While a first group of intruders faced the full battalion and later reinforcements that came in tanks from other command center, the second group was responsible for using a civilian vehicle to transport more than 500 AK-103 rifles, which immediately scaped with an unknown course.

"Come Captain, here we are, we must leave, we are surrounded and reinforcements are arriving", shouted Inspector Torres to Captain Caguantonio, leader of the operation.

"Get out, I'm hurt, I'm holding you while you escape," Torres shouted to flee, and Caguantonio didn't want to. In fact he didn't, he strangely ceased fire for some reason and furtively without leaving a trace they were able to escape having as allies the darkness of the night.

The vehicle loaded with the objective of the assault, that is, weapons, ammunition and grenades, which would serve for the freedom project, was left abandoned in an area of difficult access, after making a transfer to another vehicle. In this way the authorities found the minibus after 5 hours of the event, but absolutely empty.

In the assault as a whole, war material had been stolen to strengthen the arsenal that had gradually been built for the 2nd independence of Venezuela as it was called among the Democratic military. In total there were 500 AK-103 rifles with 500 loaders of this type of rifle, 140 grenades of 40 mm50 140 grenades of 40 mm. multiple grenade launchers of 40 mm. 80 bayonets, 60 pistols.

In the confrontation the Bolivar warriors managed to remove 8 traitors presumably from the island, while the group of brave lost 3 of the 11 members of the assault group. The weapons had been extracted without novelty and never found their whereabouts, in spite of the information offered by members of the government, who assured that they had found the lot of the material in an abandoned vehicle. Some of the dissidents who directed the seizure of the barracks were captured days later by means of betrayals and the work of the F3 of the Island, to be brutally tortured in the dungeons of the communist dictatorship that reigned on Bolivar soil.

The performance of the group of military heroes of the homeland was proportional to the desperation that the population lived at that time, wandering through the streets and queuing in the garbage cans to find something to eat, and in the best of cases, queuing in the back of any restaurant, where members and relatives of government personnel ate, to later buy the leftovers that were put on sale by the restaurants. A situation never seen before in the country whose heroes got freedom for 5 nations of the American continent.

The lack of medical supplies, antibiotics, surgical material for interventions, lack of medicines for chemo and radiotherapy, lack of milk for newborns, lack of equipment for simple X-rays, caused the general collapse of the health sector and was when it was declared in emergency. That was the pressure of the heroes of Bolivar.

Daily in the capital city died 5 newborn children on average, while the elderly died in the queues to collect a miserable pension of about 1 dollar or they passing away when they tried to withdraw money from an ATM.   Malnutrition in children was brutal, a situation that was evident in the calls for help through social networks to try to save the lives of the angels who were dying in the midst of the misfortune of that chronic invasion.

While the Captain Caguantonio was captured, the Commander Larez does not would count with the same story.
"Please you should stop, we want to surrender. Here are civilians, women and they are pregnant. There is no need to use missiles," was the exchange of words maintained by the leader and population inspiration, Omar Larez, who had also been betrayed by a close friend.

The most certain blow that the dissidence could have received was that January 15, 2018, when the most active group in the struggle for freedom was ambushed and massacred in a sector of the capital, after details of its location were known.

That war attack, through the use of mortars, grenades and war tanks for a group of 13 people, had been excessive, especially when in the middle of the operation the Group commanded by Omar Larez surrendered and with a white flag, live through different social networks, requested a Public Prosecutor, but the order of President Tomas Dabajuro was to kill Larez and the dissident group.

"We want a Public Prosecutor," Larez shouted, practically without energy, but showing courage never seen live through social networks.

"Compatriots, children of Bolivar, the freedom of our country does not depend on anyone but yourselves. All of you must go out to fight for your freedom, I know you want us dead, that's why this will be the last time you listen to me. To my kids, I love you children very much, I was fighting for our country.

Don't give up, compatriots," at that point the transmission had fallen as a result of the explosion of a missile launched by a war tank, directly to the urbanization house where the group of heroes of the homeland was located. Omar Larez and the heroes had been murdered by the Communist Dictatorship in violation of all universal codes of honor, before the surrender of a group of fighters surrendered with a white flag. The order was to kill.

From there only one thing was clear. The invading group led by Tomas Dabajuro and commanded from the Island, would only leave the South American nation without life.

Chapter 10

Finally the light arrived

"Colonel my respects I hope you are fine. Who Write is Rodolfo Vega. I communicate by this way, by text messages to avoid any interception of my messages for you. I want to tell you that I will be in the country for a few days before I leave again. I don't know if you are aware that they marked me and I can't stay freely," and pausing he sent the message to Colonel Herrera.

Rodolfo did not know why, but Colonel Herrera inspired him trust beyond the normal, he had even been closer to him, than to Don Roberto, his own father, perhaps because of the deep political differences that existed between them.

Pirulin...pirulin...'Sound of incoming message'... Rodolfo saw the screen of his smartphone and it was a voice message from the Colonel. "Greetings Rodolfo welcome. You do well to stay out of it, it's time for weapons and it's better that you contribute at the tactical level. Watch when you want to show up. You know where to find me, let's keep in touch in this way and please maintain a good level of security.If by some chance we do not speak again, take care of yourself, that you are very much appreciated. "After hearing that message, Rodolfo responded to finish the conversation:" Thank you, Colonel, we will be in touch. "

From abroad the pronouncements against the Dictatorship of Tomas Dabajuro increased, even countries that until a few months ago supported his administration now turned their backs on him, but that rejection was not free, simply the price of a barrel of oil was in free fall since 2016, even reaching 26 dollars, and that fact caused him to be left alone, because he could not buy votes in the different organizations to which the South American Nation belonged, to the same extent increased his rejection in the international community.

Not to mention the blockade that the President and the U.S. government had on him, being this factor the one that was really causing damage to the plans for the expansion of Communism in the Hemisphere, since without economic resources or trade with the countries of the area, he was soon isolating himself.

In the same international sense, the Supreme Justice Court in exile, was gradually putting the rope around the Dictator's neck, since after the Prosecutor's accusations before the International Tribunals for human rights violations, and due of the famine it was causing in the South American nation, which was also certified and endorsed by the different NGOs operating in the country, that aforementioned court of justice, had dedicated itself to raise a very specific accusation, for corruption and having received money of Odebret company.

In other words, if he wasn't caught in one way, he would be caught in the other, as happened with the famous Italian-American gangster Al Capone, whom was not possible prove his crimes, but was put behind bars for not paying his taxes.

Tomas Dabajuro and his followers of the 21st century Revolution, were slowly being fenced, especially those involved in crimes against humanity and those linked to drug trafficking and terrorism, since they do not prescribe and the Americans were implacable in this.

The north american government had not wanted to make a direct intervention, to avoid meddling in Russian or Chinese interests. Because this could have triggered a war of great proportions. On the contrary, the President of the American Empire, dedicated himself to negotiate with his counterparts, first of all from the Northern of Norea, with whom he came out with a handshake, in fact he moved peace between the North and the South of the peninsula. Then he met with the leader Sebastian Putin, to whom President Thunder had done a favor asking for the reinsertion of Kursia in the group of 8, to then define areas of operation of each Empire, and finally he was negotiating with the President of Chiran a new model of nuclear agreement to preserve global peace. After this journey, it was only a matter of the fall of the forerunners of the disaster that had the continent on edge of the disaster, because of the diaspora that was disrupting almost all the countries of America.

"Amilcar I think somebody is following me, I am pretty sure a vehicle has made 4 crossings behind me. Help me, what I do," said Rodolfo desperate for the situation.

"Who are with you Rodolfo," Amilcar asked immediately.

"I'm alone so I'm running more easily, please call the Colonel Amilcar," shouted Rodolfo as a couple of shots were heard across the line.

"Sorry Rodolfo. I'm so sorry," Amilcar said goodbye, cutting off communication.

"Amilcar that you have done....Amilcarrrr.....as you betrayed me",
yelled out Rodolfo while more shots were heard.

In one of those Rodolfo doing a maneuver with the steering wheel
was able to evade the chase, just in a street that passes next to a
high type bridge, let the car that followed him hit the bumper, and
in a movement of steering wheel managed to climb the high while
the car that followed him continued through the channel at ground
level. After this he was able to escape.

Suddenly he felt cold and realized he was bleeding. One of the
projectiles had hit him at the height of his right shoulder and he
was losing a lot of blood.
Rodolfo could not lose consciousness because if that happened
he could be a dead man. He made an effort not to faint until that
in a second he realized that he was a few blocks away from the
Hospital de Clínicas. He went there through the emergency zone
and when he arrived he fainted, but before he fell unconscious he
gave information about what happened to him. Soon family and
friends came to his aid.

Fortunately the wound had only touched the deltoid muscles on his right shoulder, so he quickly recovered. After a couple of hours in the Hospital, he was transferred to another care center at his own request, due to the fact that his persecutors could return to complete the work. Later, more relaxed he asked to be discharged because he had to leave urgently. Faced with questions of rigour on the part of the doctors, Rodolfo said that it had been to rob him, when he well knew that the reason was different.

Having everything ready for his departure trip he contacted his friend chela, to buy some tickets to Miami via Aruba, only at the time they were not purchased, not even booked. There was a plan, so she bought tickets by land to the sister Republic, to create confusion. When he arrived at the airport Chela quickly bought the first class tickets, whose availability was more feasible, and Rodolfo with his wife and children were able to board without inconvenience, at least until that time the flight to the Island of Aruba, making a stop, and with final destination the city of Miami.

Rodolfo had been saved, even when his heart was broken. As it was possible that his childhood friend, his brother Amilcar, had betrayed him in this way. He had sold it perhaps for a few dollars. That pain could not get rid of him, and only the smiling faces of his children could lift his spirits to start a new life since now he was determined not to return to the South American Republic at least while the communist dictatorship of Tomas Dabajuro controlled from the island and Paul Valastro, since about a year and a half ago, when the older dictator Joel Valastro left this world because of old age.

While Rodolfo was in Miami, his brother Benny picked him up at the airport to give him all the attention he needed. Benny knew what his brother was going through because he had experienced it firsthand when due to the videos he captured when the police shot a citizen just for protesting. From there the persecution against him began, but fortunately at that time Rodolfo had helped him to go out with his son, to ask for asylum on American soil. Fortunately, Rodolfo was known for his long career as a national and international journalist and the different friends he had left throughout his professional life offered to give him a hand in his new stage in exile. North America was a country of liberties where he wanted to be.

"Colonel I am Rodolfo", Rodolfo was telephoning his mentor to tell him what had happened.

"Fucking Rodolfo I found out what happened, how are you? Are you all right? Do you need help? Please tell me," Herrera literally told him.

"Colonel, I want to be honest with you, I find myself destroyed, my brother Amilcar has betrayed me. During the chase I managed to call him and he replied in a cold tone telling me that he felt he could do nothing. That has upset me and made me lose my faith. I don't trust anyone, Colonel," he told Herrera in a gray tone.

To all these Herrera couldn't find the way to tell him what had happened because I didn't know how Rodolfo will take it, and I was waiting for a little more tranquility and lucidity to tell him how things had happened.

"Rodolfo listens attentively to what I am going to tell you. I am going to explain to you what happened that night when you were the object of the persecution. First I want to tell you that Amilcar is dead, he was murdered by the henchmen of the dictatorship," Herrera explained quietly, while Rodolfo had had to sit down because his ears could not believe what he was hearing.

"Yes Rodolfo, Amilcar was intercepted after one of our meetings and was kidnapped for a couple of days during which he hide your location because he knew you were a marked card. He protected you until the last moment but then the tortures were too much and he gave your location", with rage in his tone of voice the Colonel explained to him how the events had occurred.

Rodolfo shouted, "But because he was captured who spoke, is anyone infiltrated? What's going on," he continued shouting through the thread. At that moment Rodolfo broke down and began to cry disconsolately because he had doubted his brother. He had thought he had sold it and it was just the opposite. Thanks to him he was able to escape and now he was safe in comfort, with his family, his wife and children. He felt that he would not be able to live with that feeling of guilt.

"By the way, Rodolfo, you know a woman named Chela Garcia," asked the Colonel, hoping that Rodolfo's answers were negative.
"Yes my Colonel she is my friend," said Rodolfo.
"I'm sorry to tell you that she also died, she was found lifeless inside her apartment", there was a silence and then Rodolfo apologizing to the Colonel cut off the communication.

Chela had been tracked through the purchase of the ticket for Rodolfo, and she was suddenly followed to her apartment where after being tortured by asphyxiation, seeking to give the exact whereabouts of Rodolfo and as she did not know, she was killed with a bullet to the head as used to do the agents of the dictatorship.

Meanwhile, in the meeting room where the military leaders of the dissidents were located, there was silence and through techniques used by the military intelligence, they managed to discover and capture the snitch responsible for Amilcar's capture and murder.

However, the most surprising thing was that the same card had been responsible for the ambush of Commissioner Omar Larez and his group in the town of 'Juntico', whom the dictatorship had massacred with an arsenal of war, in a cowardly manner after their surrender, even with shots of grace in the forehead of each one of them as revealed by forensic reports.

That discovery caused an uncontrollable uproar and the fury of those present was going to provoke their lynching. Quickly and before the lynching that had been proposed by the dissidents to avenge the death of their leader, Herrera fainted the infiltrator with an accurate blow to the jaw to avoid the lynching and at the same time subject the detainee. It was then that the Colonel, with the command voice that he maintains over his team, asked for calm, otherwise he would fall to the same level as the assassins who held power. He gave instructions to end the meeting and directions to tie up the infiltrator.

As a result of the request of names and personal data to the Banking and Financial systems at the international level by the anti-corruption commission of the National Assembly of the Republic, the entities began to offer all the data. But not only that, also the Institutions had the courtesy to offer a report, which explained that by virtue of the exorbitant sums in some accounts, they had been classified in a special line. That is to say that now if the Banks and financial networks are washing their hands around the money in those accounts knowing that its origin was doubtful. A kind of justification on the part of the Banks to absolve themselves of responsibility in the face of the fact that it was money, that it came from corruption or drug trafficking.

Along with the reports was attached a certification that all traced accounts had been immediately blocked until the governing body of the laws in the republic will order the unlocking by written order.

The importance of freezing those accounts was not only related to the repatriation of capital belonging to the people of the nation, but through these accounts could be traced to establish where the money was stolen or if it belonged to drug trafficking or to the bribes Odebret payments.

After the brutal level of corruption, looting and orchestrated invasion plan had come to light, the Dictatorship had only one ally left, whose experience in the use of force and espionage gave him the opportunity to stay in the power, especially now that the middle and troop commanders were waking up to try to rescue the Republic.

"Attorney, please come into my office," and cutting the phone line Brigadier General Jesus Armando Portillo has called Dr. Gabriel Diaz, Rodolfo's childhood friend.
"Greetings my General to your order Sir," cordially greeting Gabriel entered the office, and judging the General's face he realized once that it was no good at all, and immediately put himself on mental guard.

"Doctor I have been informed that for some time you have been frequenting the Journalist Rodolfo Vega. Why you have been talking to him and since when you don't see him," asked the General, while looking away at the monitor of his laptop, open on the desk full of papers.

"General, I know Vega because he sold me the car I currently use. As a result of there, as the car has presented some problems, we have kept in touch so that he can be responsible for some of the details, the most serious by the way. As for since when I do not see him, I can tell you that about 10 months ago I do not know about him. The last time I called him he didn't answer, and that was about 6 months ago when one of the electric fans got damaged", answered Gabriel coldly, at the same time that he asked, "My General I must know something?".

The General replied, "No Doctor nothing happens. By the way, your car is VW, isn't it? To which Rodolfo nodded as he continued to listen, "And where did you find the electric ventilator because I need one for me," ended the General.

Rodolfo more relaxed replied, "My General I found it on the Internet but it cost me an eye of the face. I will investigate, if I can find another a little cheaper, I will tell you Sir," replied Gabriel.

"Thank you Doctor, you can leave," answered the General as he picked up the phone to call the command.

Gabriel left the office of the Commander and at that time had no blood in his veins. He knew that the dissidents were being tracked and that connection to Rodolfo was critical to his person. In addition, the day before Gabriel had heard of a news story that froze the blood of all members of the Armed Forces.

The national media and analysts from the military source had made it public that a total of 2,000 members of the Armed Forces had tested positive for HIV, i.e. they had tested positive for the AIDS virus. This revelation about such a high number of military men positive to the virus, made one think that it had been induced, that is to say that the disease was provoked and that those military men had been infected with all intention.

Why is such a high numbers of soldiers revealed in one fell swoop? The military receive regular medical examinations. Why the examinations did not show the situation? Why didn't the cases appear gradually or progressively, as regularly happens in cases of epidemics of this type? or Why does this happen at times when the sabres sound against the communist dictatorship?

All those questions only found an answer, and was not other that to get rid of the military whose patriotic attitude put at risk the welfare of the dictatorship and the invasion executed step by step from the Island. In that way they had the free way to replace those contingents, with more agents infiltrated from the island without arousing suspicions or in the best of cases with young people who did not have the slightest idea of what democracy meant in the country. In other words, they only knew communism as system of life.

This blow to the possible liberators of the homeland was given just at the moment prior to a coordinated action from the heart of dissidence, for which it was presumed again another infiltration in the ranks loyal to the people.

But how could they have infiltrated all sectors of society? And from where did the Dictatorship get resources to pay the infiltrated cards, knowing that the blockades promoted by the North American government and attended at an international level, had economically isolated the regime.

The answer was found in drug trafficking, and in the extraction of minerals in an excessive way, that were immediately traded on the black market, speaking in terms of gold as well as diamonds. On a smaller scale, Coltan and Thorum, because they are minerals with more specific uses, but Asian companies in the area would be making juicy profits with their extraction.

But what about Uranium. Which had happened with the extraction of such a dangerous mineral, whose use by wrong hands could create a catastrophe on the planet?

From the moment the international organizations focused their gaze on the South American country, and from the moment the neighboring country of the south changed government and whose policies were not aligned with those of communism. The extraction was stopped at least temporarily. It was drug trafficking and gold, the black economy that was maintaining the activities of a government that was in marked decline.

The team made by the Maximum Court of Justice, the Attorney General of the Republic, from exile, as well as the National Assembly from the Capital of the Republic, had been perfect in the sense of working in harmony in order to carry out actions to restore constitutional order in the country.

There were different options to judge Tomas Dabajuro and among the evidence obtained from the files that rested in the seat of the Prosecution, and that were stolen by the Prosecutor Ortigoza Friaz before his film style escape, was one especially appropriate according to the jurists of the maximum governing body of justice. This was the one related to the acts of corruption that Dabajuro had committed repeatedly, from his time as chancellor of the late Lugo Galvez, to even after having reached the presidency.

This evidence was ideal for building the case that would allow him to be tried and sentenced, since the plot involved several countries in the area, including at the European level. These international ramifications of corruption, were going to allow to activate the Convention of the United Nations against the transnational crime, also called "Convention of Palermo", which had as purpose to establish parameters for the international application of the laws homologating domestic aspects of each country to punish in this way the organized crime. This convention had been signed at the end of the year two thousand in the Italian city of Palermo and was signed by 124 of 189 member countries of the United Nations.

"I want to get out of this problem, but how?", were the textual words pronounced by President Tomas Dabajuro speaking in a concerned manner with the first combatant about the actions that would follow, since the fence was getting smaller and smaller.

"Tomas we're in this and we can't get out now. We must continue, some way out will appear. If we flee now no one will receive us. We don't have any money because everything is blocked. We can't even count on the gold we repatriated, because you came up with the brilliant idea of listening to Joel and Paul, and we sent them to the Island.

Now, how do you think we're going to ask for the gold. It's from the Island where the orders come not to abandon, to maintain calm, because international military intervention will not be carried out," said Lilia staring at the floor, as if looking for some element to wield it as a possible salvation tablet.

"On the other hand, if at least we show that we want to disappear, Diogenes kills us, because that is precisely what he wants to

become the savior of the people in the midst of this disaster that has formed," she finished expressing her ideas, rubbing both hands as if the cold entered his body, but they were the nerves that had them both sick.

Another issue was that of his nephews, who were paying jail for wanting to bring almost a ton of drugs into Uncle Sam's house.
That situation had thrown Lilia Sores the First Combatant, the warrior. It was no longer the same, she was practically sedated 24 hours a day to be able to bear the torment of remembering her nephews, practically children, locked up and so far away. She did not even have the consolation of being able to visit them because in doing so they could also leave her detained for so much damage done to the South American Republic.

Tun...tun...tun...(Sound of door and fright!) "President chain in 10 minutes", it was the aide of guard who entered to warn that he had to prepare for another allocution through Television.
This was the key to how the Dictator Dabajuro appeared to have control of everything, with three television cameras, the support of 5 Generals and the strongest groups of collectives in the Capital. However, little by little the people realized how fragile a dictatorship was, which was slowly running out of options.

The chain was obligatory to try to intimidate the people that every day went out with more frequency and in greater quantity to protest due to the lack of food, of medicine or of electrical energy. The Dictatorship no longer had anything to support themselves.

To the existing tense situation, a devaluation of the undeclared currency was added, with the elimination of five zeros, which kept the population permanently altered.

The hours were decisive because the announcement of an increase in the price of fuel had been made, and that was a taboo subject, since that would have been the excuse for the 1989 'Carajazo'.

Now it was up to the worst President in the history of the Republic to announce the official amount of the new price of gasoline and because of the winds that blew, it was not going to please a population that was looking for any pretext to die in the street, since the other option was to die or to see their children die of hunger, diseases or without electricity in the country. What would the Maximum Court of Justice do about it?

The mettle of the members of that Maximum Court of Justice in exile was steel. They had received death threats against them and their family members. In fact, two of the magistrates chose not to participate in the trial against Dictator Tomas Dabajuro, due to the fact that they had family members registered in national territory, who could not leave in time.

In recent days, the National Assembly of the Republic approved the commencement of the trial process. Using as headquarters and protected by the majesty of the Congress of the Columbia, the Maximum Court of Justice legally sworn in its opportunity by the National Assembly, began the public trial transmitted live to the entire planet.

It was loaded with physical evidence in addition to documents, videos and audios relating to the misdeeds and acts of corruption carried out by the current President of the Republic through the company Odebret, even since his time as chancellor next to Lugo Galvez.

The Court formally and verifiably accused citizen Tomas Dabajuro Toro, on whom the prosecutor had requested the maximum sentence of 30 years in prison. Then the defendant's defense made its presentation, obviously with the defendant in absence. The defence lawyer worked on the innocence of the person he represented, arguing that at no time had his client had access to any of the representatives of the company in question and that, consequently, the evidence presented lacked veracity. The trial proceeded as planned, with only the sentence missing to disclose the guilt or innocence of the accused, which is why a ninety-minute recess was established before the final sentence was handed down, in a trial that would set a unique precedent in world legal history, speaking in international terms.

After the pause the Maximum Court of Justice taking its respective location in the Palace of the laws of the Columbia Congress, read and sentenced.

"This plenary of the Maximum Court of Justice has sufficiently proven with full evidence, the commission of the punishable acts object of this investigation and a causality that demonstrates reliably the culpability and criminal responsibility of Tomas Dabajuro Toro in the perpetration of own corruption and legitimation of Capitals", the sentence had been read by one of the members of the court.

"Consequently, citizen Tomas Dabajuro Toro is sentenced to serve a prison term of 18 years and 3 months, in the El Verde Region prison, and he must also pay a fine of 25 million dollars for the crime of corruption and for the crime of money laundering, he must compensate the Republic for the amount of 35 billion dollars," finalized the member of the court in charge of reading the sentence, while the President of the Court declared the session closed.

In those days when everything was in turmoil. Soldiers wielding sabres in the barracks, hunger and scarcity of medicine among the population, with burned nights, people protesting and explosions caused by the general darkness due to the lack of electric service and even more by the sentence of guilt of the President. Anyone could think that everything was ready for the fall of the regime, but the stamina shown by the bandits was monumental, and the more the fence was closed over them, the more they assaulted, for which only 24 hours after the jail sentence for the President, this one in nationwide TV transmission, announced a series of measures to bankrupting the country, taking away institutions and companies. A minimum wage went from 6 million bolívares to 180 million bolívares a month, which meant that the economic devastation could have no other description than the 'Intentional Bankruptcy' of the nation.

The Isleño F3 then began to apply its techniques and strategies to unveil the plans of dissidence, and behind the spearhead of 6 audios that ran like gunpowder through the social networks, affirming that the Maximum Court of Justice had dismissed the President and appointed his successor.

This in a normal situation would have caused the group of military honorable men to emerge, but the Dictatorship for 20 years showed and taught so much that the military liberators and the flannel soldiers in the streets did not fell in the trap.

BREAKING NEWS: "An strong earthquake off the coast of the South American Republic was confirmed this Tuesday afternoon, with an intensity of 7.3 on the Richter scale. The telluric movement was felt from the eastern coasts of the country crossing all the national Territory, until being felt in the neighboring country Columbia. From the Capital there are reports of damage to various structures, but miraculously there are no victims to regret. For the first time in history an Earthquake above 7 in Richter's measurement, leaves no human losses. Replicas of the event are expected, so it's recommended that the population be alert to any similar eventuality.

The news of that earthquake circled the world, due to the fact that even with the intensity of the shake, the all-powerful God of an extremely Christian Catholic nation, had not allowed the South American Republic to pass a catastrophe of the kind.

The Christian Catholic population, whose percentage was almost 70 percent, attributed the seismic event to a miracle of liberation of the homeland, judging by the real and divine facts that had coincided in time and space. And it is that the witchcraft and black magic that had brought the colonizers of the Island in order to perform spells and ties based on the dark and animal sacrifices, had brought a kind of curse to a nation that had been characterized throughout its history for being a believer and also Christian.

The later replicas would be of lesser intensity, so that according to the most believers, the damage had already left the bowels of the homeland of Bolivar.

Time passed with his great and well-known tic...tac...tic...tic...tac...tic...tac...tac...

And one morning, when the world was attentive to any of the madnesses of the Dictator Dabajuro and his followers, on a national and later international TV transmission, Colonel Antonio Herrera announced the fall of the regime of the 21st century Revolution and its promoters on the Island, product of the detention and extraction of the leaders of this international criminal gang, whose worst mistake was to underestimate the capacity for action of the international forces, supported by the Palermo Convention, which authorized the governments of the world to recover the law in any of the signatory countries of this pact, where the constitutional thread had been lost and covered in the sentence against the Dictator Tomas Dabajuro Toro, the law could work in favor of a dying population submerged in the biggest holocaust after the one executed by Hitler during the 2nd World War.

When the patriots commanded by Colonel Herrera less announced it, they began to eliminate sentries in each one of the barracks of the Republic, and using the weapons stolen a few months before Fort Paracay, and from different military control points in several areas of the country. They subdued the middle commanders who continued to support the murderous regime.

Those weapons in hands of the invaders, which had been kidnapped for 20 years, once again served the population of Simon Bolivar. With the cry of "Vuelvan caras", The Sudamerican Republic, achieved it's second independence from foreign domination and as a consequence, once again freed the countries in whose territory the macabre communist project had wanted to expand.

Epilogue

After 20 years of crimes, damage to national patrimony, institutions and the population, with a malnourished childhood as well as illness, reconstruction was not going to be easy. But the courage and intelligence of a people who were subjected to the homolodor, that is to say, submission through hunger, could do more than the weapons and evil that came from other latitudes.

From that moment onwards, the democratic and civilized world learned to be on its guard to suddenly detect any attempt of future domination from one nation to another through indoctrination and submission, either through hunger or drugs, creating more international laws and conventions such as the Palermo Convention, which would allow cooperation, to avoid touching the extremes reached by the South American Nation.

The creation a 'posteriori' of a chair of high studies in different Universities of the world called 'Case Venezuela', would be the best way to explain in detail, the events around the Invasion of which progressively and silently had been object a country of the world.

Since 1961, there had been internal complicity in the homeland of Bolivar to support the invading project of communism. Not by a guess did the great International Television Presenter Renny Ottolina, many times he showed it, he said it clearly and abruptly as the Creole liked it. Possibly that was the fact that led him to death, when he was killed in that plane that crashed or somebody crashed it.

Due of events like this and so many others, the current political actors cannot guide the people of Bolivar towards progress. Men like Caguantonio, or like Larez were and are the ones indicated for the people to follow them. Perhaps one is dead and the other almost destroyed for pleasure. Have you ever wondered why political leaders have not been assassinated in Venezuela?

This question remains as a task for the new generations. The youth must read and be instructed with the truth about the facts of history and understand that the Third Industrial Revolution, as is the era of technology, buried in the past models and stream of thought and destroyed the hook called 'Exploitation of man by man'.

The technological age forms a man seen as a unit of production that is part of an absolute gear.

A man who works according to the tools of the knowledge he acquires in his academic formation, totally independent of employers or governments or private companies, he works and gets what he wants and when he wants.

The Case of the South American Nation will be remembered by history as the perfect formula of evasion of international laws, and let us be careful because any night of full moon in any coast of any country, could initiate another Silent Invasion...